STO

The BIG INDIANA REPRODUCIBLE Activity Book!

BY CAROLE MARSH

This activity book has material which correlates with
Indiana's Academic Standards.

At every opportunity, we have tried to relate information to
the History and Social Science, English, Science, Math, Civics,
Economics, and Computer Technology academic standards.

For additional information, go to our websites:
www.indianaexperience.com or **www.gallopade.com**.

The Big Activity Book Team

Billie Walburn

Michael Marsh

Antoinette Miller

Michele Yother

Carole Marsh

Bob Longmeyer

William Nesbitt, Jr.

Lisa Stanley

Sherry Moss

Cecil Anderson

Chad Beard

Jackie Clayton

Terry Briggs

Karin Petersen

Kathy Zimmer   Wanda Coats   Cranston Davenport   Jill Sanders

Gallopade is proud to be a member of these educational organizations and associations:

Published by

GALLOPADE™
INTERNATIONAL

800-536-2GET
www.gallopade.com

SHOPA MEMBER™
School, Home, & Office Products Association

NSSEA

ASCD

The Indiana Experience Series

The Indiana Experience! Paperback Book

My First Pocket Guide to Indiana!

The Big Indiana Reproducible Activity Book

The Indiana Coloring Book!

My First Book About Indiana!

Indiana Jeopardy: Answers and Questions About Our State

Indiana "Jography!": A Fun Run Through Our State

The Indiana Experience! Sticker Pack

The Indiana Experience! Poster/Map

Discover Indiana CD-ROM

Indiana "GEO" Bingo Game

Indiana "HISTO" Bingo Game

A Word From The Author

Indiana is a very special state. Almost everything about Indiana is interesting and fun! It has a remarkable history that helped create the great nation of America. Indiana enjoys an amazing geography of incredible beauty and fascination. The state's people are unique and have accomplished many great things.

This Activity Book is chock-full of activities to entice you to learn more about Indiana. While completing mazes, dot-to-dots, word searches, coloring activities, word codes, and other fun-to-do activities, you'll learn about Indiana's history, geography, people, places, animals, legends, and more.

Whether you're sitting in a classroom, stuck inside on a rainy day, or—better yet—sitting in the back seat of a car touring the wonderful state of Indiana, my hope is that you have as much fun using this Activity Book as I did writing it.

Enjoy your Indiana Experience—it's the trip of a lifetime!!

Carole Marsh

Color Me!

BROWN
Like the bark of the tulip tree
Brown

BLUE
Like the Indiana sky
Blue

BLACK
Like the stripes of the honeybee
Black

YELLOW
Like ripe corn on the cob
Yellow

PURPLE
Like the native violet
Purple

RED
Like the peony
Red

GREEN
Like the grassy fields
Green

ORANGE
Like pumpkins in the fall
Orange

Indiana

Geographic Tools

Beside each geographic need listed, put the initials of the tool that can best help you!

(CR) Compass Rose   (LL) Longitude and Latitude
(M) Map   (G) Grid
(K) Map key/legend

1. _____ I need to find the geographic location of Germany.

2. _____ I need to learn where an airport is located near Indianapolis

3. _____ I need to find which way is north.

4. _____ I need to chart a route from Indiana to California.

5. _____ I need to find a small town on a map.

Match the items on the left with the items on the right.

1. Grid system   A. Map key or legend
2. Compass rose   B. Illinois and Kentucky
3. Longitude and latitude   C. A system of letters and numbers
4. Two of Indiana's borders   D. Imaginary lines around the earth
5. Symbols on a map   E. Shows N, S, E, and W

ANSWERS: 1.LL 2.K 3.CR 4.M 5.G 1.C 2.E 3.D 4.B 5.A

Our State Bird!

Connect the dots to see Indiana's beautiful state bird, the Cardinal.

When you are done, color the bird.

Write the bird's name in the space below.

Male Cardinals are bright red, and females are light brown.

The Cardinal is the only red bird with a crest!

Cardinals eat grapes, holly berries, and blackberries.

They lay eggs that are pale bluish white with little brown spots.

– – – – – – – – –

Mounds Abound in Indiana!

People have lived in Indiana for thousands of years. One group of people, called the Mississippians or Mound Builders, lived on the banks of the Ohio River from about 1100 to 1450. They built big earthen mounds shaped like beehives, and one of their villages was near present-day Evansville. It's called Angel Mounds after a man named Mathias Angel who once owned the land. Several thousand people lived there. A stockade made of branches and mud was built around the village to protect the village and the chief. Nobody knows why, but the Mound Builders deserted the village hundreds of years ago.

Pretend that you are an archaeologist digging into one of the Indiana mounds. Below are pictures of some of the artifacts that you find. Now, you have to identify these strange objects and their uses. Write down what you think these things are for!

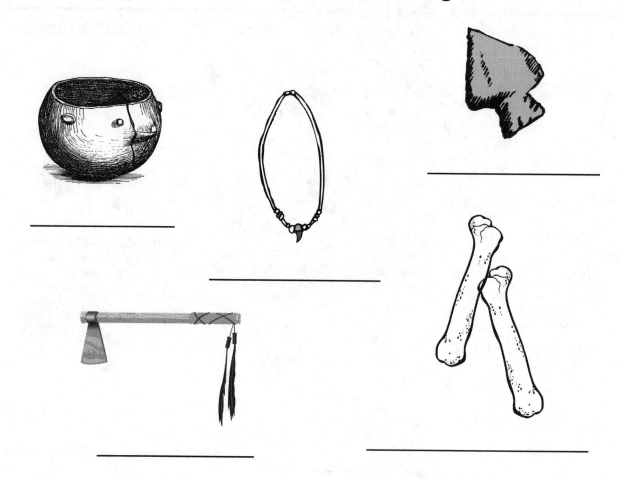

Local Government

Indiana's state government, just like our national government, is made up of three branches. Each branch has a certain job to do. Each branch also has some power over the other branches. We call this system checks and balances. The three branches work together to make our government run smoothly.

Match each of the professionals with their branch.

This branch is made up of the General Assembly which has two houses, the Senate and the House of Representatives. This branch makes and repeals laws.	This branch includes the government leaders made up of the governor, as well as appointed and elected state officials. This branch makes sure that the laws are enforced.	This branch includes the court system, which consists of the local, district, and state courts. This branch interprets the laws.
A. Legislative Branch	**B. Executive Branch**	**C. Judicial Branch**

1. the governor ____

2. a local district representative ____

3. a senator ____

4. an appointed trustee of a state university ____

5. the chief justice of the State Supreme Court ____

6. the speaker of the House of Representatives ____

7. the lieutenant governor ____

8. appellate court judge ____

9. a district attorney ____

10. a member of the General Assembly ____

Vote for me in 2008!

ANSWERS: 1.B 2.A 3.A 4.B 5.C 6.A 7.B 8.C 9.B 10.A

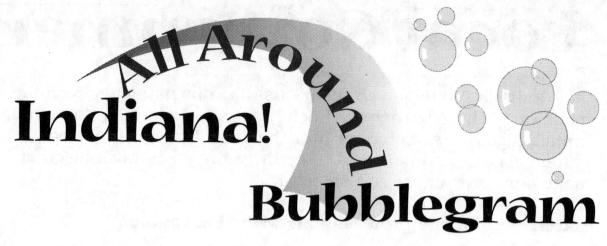

All Around Indiana! Bubblegram

Bubble up on your knowledge of Indiana's bordering states and bodies of water.

Fill in the bubblegram by using the clues below.

1. A state west of Indiana
2. A state south of Indiana
3. A state north of Indiana
4. The capital of Indiana
5. Indiana's state river

1. _ _ _ _ Ⓞ _ _ _

2. _ Ⓞ _ _ _ _ _ _

3. _ _ _ Ⓞ _ _ _ _

4. _ _ _ _ _ _ _ _ Ⓞ _ _ Ⓞ _

5. _ _ _ Ⓞ _ _ _

Now unscramble the "bubble" letters to discover the mystery word.
HINT: What is Indiana's nick name?

MYSTERY WORD: _ _ _ _ _ _ R

Symbols of the United States

These are some of the symbols that remind us of America. We show these symbols honor and respect.

Color each symbol.

American Flag

Statue of Liberty

Bald Eagle

Liberty Bell

Hoosier Holes!

In southern Indiana it is common to see caves and caverns (especially large caves). The natural acids in rain and snow worked to dissolve the limestone underground to form hollowed-out caves and underground streams. Bluespring Cavern, near Bedford, is one of the ten largest caves in the world. Most of the cavern's miles are underground streams, and it's home to the longest "lost river" in the country. Wyandotte Cave, near Leavenworth, is one of the largest caves in North America. It has more than 35 miles (56 kilometers) of underground passageways.

Marengo Cave, north of Wyandotte Cave, houses a magnificent underground room called the Crystal Palace. Underground weddings and dances in the cave have been common over the years. Each July, a square dance is held in the cave's Music Hall Chamber!

The Squire Boone Caverns, near Corydon, were discovered by Daniel Boone and his brother Squire. Squire settled in the area, and when he died, he was buried in the cavern. Squire Boone Caverns contain a wonderful mix of colorful stalactites and stalagmites, and underground streams and waterfalls; no wonder it's been called the most dazzling cave around!

Pretend that you are a "spelunker" (person who explores caves). What sort of tools do you think you'd need to thoroughly investigate a cave? Circle the tools you'd need below.

Indiana Wheel of Fortune, Indian Style!

The names of Indiana's many Native American tribes contain enough consonants to play . . . Wheel of Fortune!

See if you can figure out the Wheel of Fortune-style puzzles below! "Vanna" has given you some of the consonants in each word.

Two Brothers and Tippecanoe, Too!

In 1808, two Native American brothers named Tecumseh and Tenskwatawa RELOCATED to the area near the Tippecanoe River in Indiana. Tenskwatawa was called the "Shawnee Prophet" because he preached to several Indian groups. Tecumseh also spoke to many Indians, ENCOURAGING them to organize and resist the European settlers who were taking their land.

Tecumseh traveled all over, trying to UNITE the tribes into a confederacy against the settlers. Meanwhile, Tenskwatawa led a group of Indians in the Battle of Tippecanoe. On November 7, 1811, General William Henry Harrison CLASHED with the Prophet near his village, and the Prophet lost. Tenskwatawa lost many men, and Tecumseh's hopes for a united Indian confederacy were DASHED.

See if you can figure out the meanings of these words from the story

1. relocated:_____

2. encouraging: _____

3. unite: _____

4. clashed: _____

5. dashed: _____

Now check your answers in a dictionary. How close did you get to the real definitions?

Rainbow, Pretty Rainbow

Rainbows often appear over the Ohio River after a storm. Rainbows are the brightest, most beautiful rainbows. You can see rainbows early or late on a rainy day when the sun is behind you.

Color the rainbow in the order the colors are listed below, starting at the top of the rainbow.

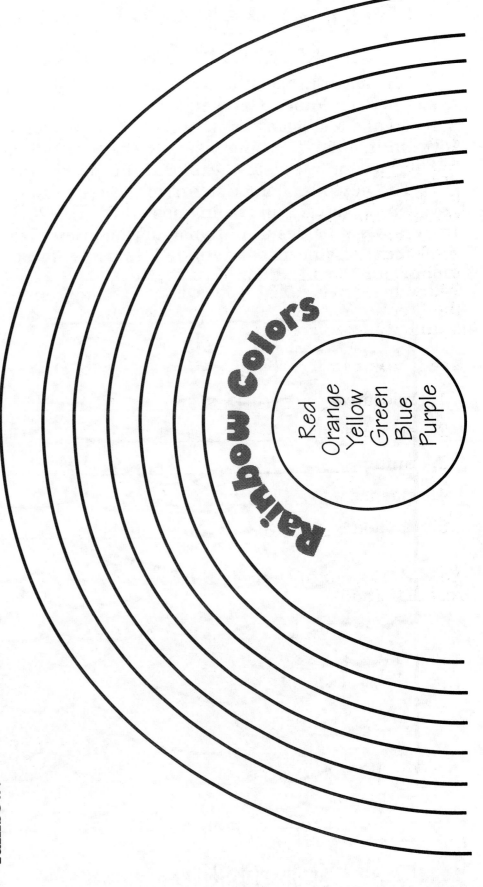

Rainbow Colors

Red
Orange
Yellow
Green
Blue
Purple

In the Beginning...
Came the French

The first European to come to Indiana was the French explorer René-Robert Cavelier, Sieur de La Salle. He sailed across Lake Michigan from Canada in 1679, to the St. Joseph River in Indiana. He hoped to find a way to sail all the way to the Pacific Ocean, but instead explored northern Indiana.

The next Frenchmen to arrive were fur traders, often called voyageurs, who set up trading posts in the 1720s. Following the fur traders were the Jesuit Catholic missionaries. They founded the settlement of Vincennes around 1732. **Help La Salle find his way from Canada to Indiana!**

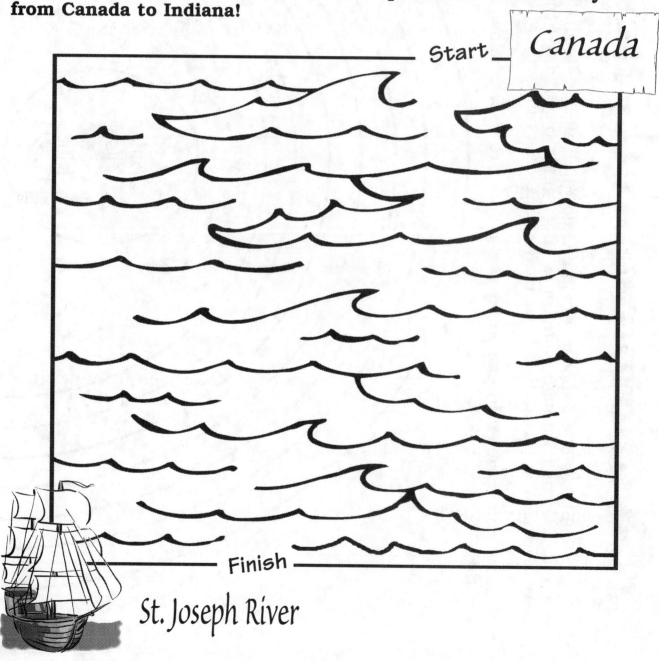

Start _ Canada

Finish

St. Joseph River

U.S. Time Zones

Would you believe that the contiguous United States is divided into four time zones? It is! Because of the rotation of the earth, the sun travels from east to west. When the sun is directly overhead, we call that time noon. When it's noon in Indianapolis, the sun has a long way to go before it's directly over San Francisco, California.

Indiana is actually split between two different time zones, and most Indianans don't change their clocks during Daylight Savings Time! Ten Indiana counties (near Chicago, Illinois and Evansville) are in the Central Time Zone, and five (near Cincinnati, Ohio and Louisville, Kentucky) are in the Eastern Time Zone. The other 77 counties are on Eastern Standard Time all year. When it's noon (12:00 p.m.) in Clarksville (near Louisville), it's actually 11:00 a.m. in Evansville!

Look at the time zones on the map below, then answer the following questions:

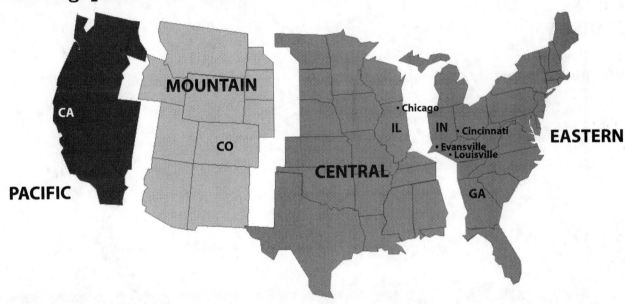

1. When it is 10:00 a.m. in Corydon (near Louisville, Kentucky) what time is it in California? _____ a.m.

2. When it is 3:30 p.m. in Atlanta, Georgia what time is it in Gary, Indiana (near Chicago, Illinois)? _____ p.m.

3. In what time zone(s) is Indiana located? _____

4. In what time zone is Colorado located? _____

5. If it is 10:00 p.m. in Evansville, Indiana what time is it in Colorado? _____ p.m.

Sing Like a Indiana Bird
Word Jumble!

Arrange the jumbled letters in the proper order for the names of birds found in Indiana.

BLUE JAY
CARDINAL
CROW
GOOSE
GROUSE
PHEASANT
ROBIN
SPARROW
QUAIL
WOODPECKER

N I D L A R A C _ _ _ _ _ _ _ _

L U Q A I _ _ _ _ _

O E S O G _ _ _ _ _

R O W C _ _ _ _

S P R R W O A _ _ _ _ _ _ _

B E U L A J Y _ _ _ _ _ _ _

H P T A A E S N _ _ _ _ _ _ _ _

S E R O G U _ _ _ _ _ _

D O O W P C E E K R _ _ _ _ _ _ _ _ _ _

B I N O R _ _ _ _ _

Some Patriotic Holidays

FLAG DAY

Flag Day is celebrated on June 14 to honor our flag. Our country's flag is an important symbol. It makes us proud of our country. It makes us proud to be Americans.

Count the number of stars and stripes on the flag.

_____ Stars   _____ Stripes

MEMORIAL DAY

Memorial Day is also known as Decoration Day. We remember the people who died in wars and fought so that we could be free.

Circle the things you might put on a grave on Memorial Day.

VETERANS DAY

On Veterans Day we recognize Americans who served in the armed forces.

Circle ways we celebrate Veterans Day.

Indiana Schools Rule!

Indiana's 1816 state constitution was the first in America to provide for a system of free public schools all the way to the university level. Today, about one-half of all Indiana college students are enrolled in state-supported colleges and universities. The Indiana University system is the largest, and its main campus is in Bloomington. Many of the private universities and colleges in Indiana are affiliated with religious groups. The University of Notre Dame, was founded in 1842 by Roman Catholics. Earlham College was started in 1847 by a group of Quakers. By the 1990s, Indiana had 28 public and 68 private colleges and universities.

Complete the names of these Indiana schools. Use the Word Bank to help you. Then, use the answers to solve the code at the bottom.

WORD BANK
- **Purdue**
- **Ball State**
- **Hulman**
- **Valparaiso**
- **Notre Dame**

1. __ __ __ __ __ __ __ __ University in Muncie
   (4) (7)

2. University of __ __ __ __ __ __ __ __ __ in South Bend
   (5)

3. __ __ __ __ __ __ University in West Lafayette
   (1)

4. Rose-__ __ __ __ __ __ Institute of Technology in Terre Haute
   (6)

5. __ __ __ __ __ __ __ __ __ University in Valparaiso
   (3)   (2)

The coded message tells you what all college students want.

__ __ __ __ __ __ __
1 2 3 4 5 6 7

Getting There From Here!

Methods of transportation have changed in Indiana from the early days of explorers and settlers to the present time.

Match each person to the way they would travel.

Native American

race car driver

child

settler

astronaut

early explorer

pilot

Getting Into Indiana!

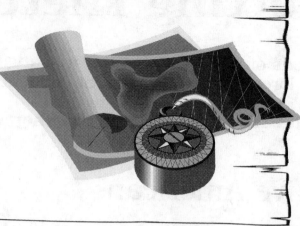

When we learn about Indiana's geography, we use special words to describe it. These words describe the things that make each part of the state interesting.

See if you can match these geographical terms with their definitions!

1. ridge

2. glacier

3. tributary

4. region

5. mound

6. lowland

7. moraine

8. strait

9. plain

10. cavern

A. a high ridge formed by melting glaciers

B. a range of hills

C. a pile or heap of earth

D. a narrow body of water joining two larger ones

E. an especially large cave

F. a river or stream that flows into a larger body of water

G. an area of land

H. a large mass of ice that moves very slowly down a mountain or across land until it melts

I. an area of land that is lower than the land around it

J. a large stretch of flat land

ANSWERS: 1.B 2.H 3.F 4.G 5.C 6.I 7.A 8.D 9.J 10.E

Oh! Say Can You See...
Indiana's State Flag

Indiana's General Assembly adopted the state flag in 1917 as part of the 1916 Indiana centennial celebration. The flag has a blue background. A golden torch in the center symbolizes liberty and enlightenment. The golden rays around the torch show how they have a wide influence. Thirteen stars circle the torch, standing for the original 13 states. The five stars near the torch's handle symbolize the states that were admitted to the Union before Indiana. The star just above the torch's flame, and the word "Indiana" above it, stand for Indiana, the 19th state.

Color Indiana's state flag.

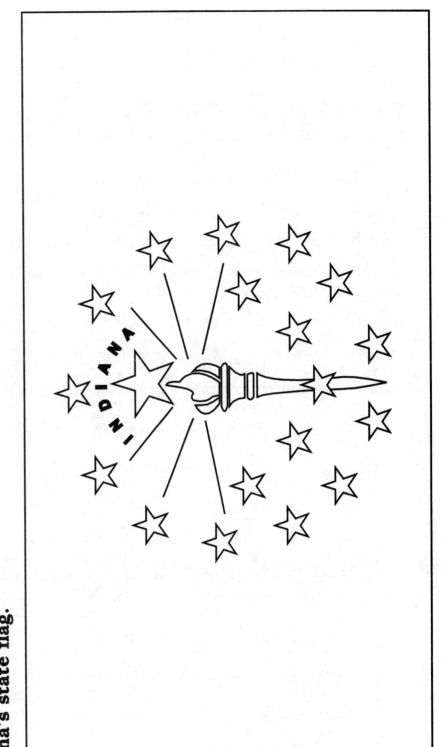

Design your own Diamante on Indiana!

A *diamante* is a diamond-shaped poem on any subject.

You can write your very own diamante poem on Indiana by following the simple line by line directions below. Give it a try!

Line 1:   Write the name of your state.

Line 2:   Write the names of two animals native to your state.

Line 3:   Write the names of three of your state's important cities.

Line 4:   Write the names of four of your state's important industries or agricultural products.

Line 5:   Write the names of your state bird, flower, and rock.

Line 6:   Write the names of two of your state's landforms.

Line 7:   Write the word that completes this sentence: Indiana's nickname is the _____ State.

_____

_____ _____

_____ _____ _____

_____ _____ _____ _____

_____ _____ _____

_____ _____

_____

James Whitcomb Riley was known as the Hoosier Poet!

He was born in a two-room log cabin in Greenfield.

Indiana, The Hoosier State!

Match the name of each Indiana state symbol on the left with its picture on the right.

State Bird

State Seal

State Flower

Tulip Tree

State Tree

State Seal

Cardinal

State Flag

State Flag

Peony

Who's a "Hoosier"?

Indianans have been called "Hoosiers" for more than 150 years, making "Hoosier" one of the oldest state nicknames in the nation! There are actually several explanations of where the term came from. Here are a few:

1. When visitors knocked on pioneers' doors in the early days of Indiana settlement, the settler would often yell "Who's yere?" "Who's yere" then became "Hoosier."

2. Indiana rivermen were so good at winning brawls, or "hushing" their opponents, that they became known as "hushers." "Husher" then turned into "Hoosier."

3. A man named Hoosier who worked on the Louisville and Portland Canal liked to hire workers from Indiana. His workers were known as "Hoosier's men," which then was shortened to "Hoosiers."

Which explanation do you think is closest to the actual origin of the word "Hoosier"? Write down the number of the explanation you prefer (1, 2, or 3), and then a couple of sentences about why you think it's probably the right one.

Explanation I think is right: _____

Reasons why I think it's right:

_____

_____

_____

_____

_____

The Bald Eagle Riddle!

The bald eagle is a national symbol of the United States.

Read the riddle and name each part of the bald eagle using words from the Word Bank.

1. I keep the eagle warm and dry. **I** am brown on the eagle's body and wings. **I** am white on the eagle's head and tail.
What am I?_____

2. I help the eagle stand and wade in shallow water to catch fish as they swim past.
What am I?_____

3. I am the eagle's home. Sometimes **I** measure 12 feet (3.6 meters) across.
What am I?_____

4. I help the eagle fly high into the sky. **I** measure 7 to 8 feet (2 to 2.4 meters) across.
What am I? _____

5. I am yellow. **I** help the eagle catch and eat fish.
What am I?_____

WORD BANK

nest   wings   beak
talons   feathers

ANSWERS: 1. feathers 2. talons 3. nest 4. wings 5. beak

What in the World?

A hemisphere is one-half of a sphere (globe) created by the prime meridian or equator. Every place in the world is in two hemispheres (Northern or Southern and Eastern or Western). The equator is an imaginary line that runs around the world from left to right and divides the globe into the Northern Hemisphere and Southern Hemisphere. Indiana is in the Northern Hemisphere.

The prime meridian is an imaginary line that runs around the world from top to bottom and divides the globe into the Eastern Hemisphere and Western Hemisphere. Indiana is in the Western Hemisphere.

Label the Eastern and Western Hemispheres.

Write PM on the prime meridian.

Color the map.

Label the Northern and Southern Hemispheres.

Write E on the equator.

Color the map.

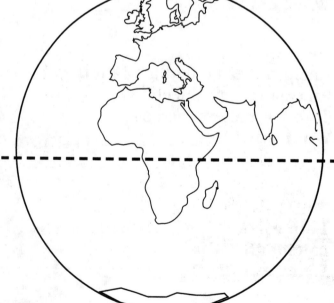

Interesting Indiana Places to go! Things to do!

1. Visit the state capitol building in _ _ _ _ _ _ _ _ _ _ _ _ _,
   and maybe even say "hi" to the governor!

2. See the enormous mosaic "Touchdown Jesus", and get a head
   start on your education, at the University of _ _ _ _ _ Dame
   in South Bend.

3. The Menno-Hof Mennonite-Amish _ _ _ _ _ _ _ _ Center
   in Shipshewana is a great place to get started on learning about
   the Amish.

4. The Auburn-Cord-Duesenberg Museum in _ _ _ _ _ _ has
   many classic Duesenberg cars.

5. The world's largest private collection of Abraham _ _ _ _ _ _ _
   memorabilia can be found in Fort Wayne.

6. At _ _ _ _ _ _ Prairie in Noblesville, it's always the year 1836.

7. _ _ _ _ _ _ _ _ _ _ is the home of the George Rogers Clark
   National Historical Park.

8. Go hiking and horseback riding in the _ _ _ _ _ County
   State Park.

WORD BANK

- Visitors
- Auburn
- Indianapolis
- Brown
- Vincennes
- Conner
- Notre
- Lincoln

Please Come to Indiana!

You have a friend who lives in Arkansas. She is thinking of moving to Indiana because she's a big sports fan. She's heard about the incredible college and professional basketball and football teams in the state, and the Indianapolis 500. You want to convince her to come to Indiana.

Write her a letter describing Indiana and some of sports events she can attend.

_____
_____
_____
_____
_____
_____
_____
_____
_____
_____
_____
_____
_____
_____
_____
_____
_____
_____
_____
_____
_____
_____

The Indianapolis Motor Speedway was built in 1909 from 3,200,000 paving bricks. It has been the home of the Indianapolis 500 race every Memorial Day since 1911. The race is 500 miles (805 kilometers) long, and it takes 200 laps around the 2.5-mile (4-kilometer) racetrack to complete it!

The Underground Railroad

Although the French and early American settlers from the South brought black slaves into Indiana, Indiana's 1816 state constitution prohibited slavery. In fact, the 1851 state constitution made it illegal for blacks to even enter the state! Many Indianans wanted to help slaves who were escaping from the South, and joined the Underground Railroad.

The Underground Railroad was a secret network of people and places that helped slaves travel safely from southern states to freedom in the North. Many of the people were Quakers. Levi Coffin of Fountain City helped as many as 2,000 slaves on their way to Canada. Fountain City, which was a Quaker community, became known as the Grand Central Station of the Underground Railroad!

Use information from the story above to complete the crossword.

1. Thousands of slaves passed through _____ City. (ACROSS)
2. Levi _____ helped as many as 2,000 slaves on their way to Canada. (DOWN)
3. Fountain City was a _____ community. (DOWN)
4. Slaves wanted to _____ to the North. (ACROSS)
5. Fountain City was called the Grand Central Station of the Underground _____road. (DOWN)

ANSWERS: 1.Fountain 2.Coffin 3.Quaker 4.escape 5.rail

Indiana Rules!

Use the code to complete the sentences.

A̲ B̲ C̲ D̲ E̲ F̲ G̲ H̲ I̲ J̲ K̲ L̲ M̲ N̲ O̲ P̲ Q̲ R̲ S̲ T̲ U̲ V̲ W̲ X̲ Y̲ Z̲
1 2 3 4 5 6 7 8 9 10 11 12 13 14 15 16 17 18 19 20 21 22 23 24 25 26

1. State rules are called $\frac{}{12}\ \frac{}{1}\ \frac{}{23}\ \frac{}{19}$.

2. Laws are made in our state $\frac{}{3}\ \frac{}{1}\ \frac{}{16}\ \frac{}{9}\ \frac{}{20}\ \frac{}{15}\ \frac{}{12}$.

3. The leader of our state is the $\frac{}{7}\ \frac{}{15}\ \frac{}{22}\ \frac{}{5}\ \frac{}{18}\ \frac{}{14}\ \frac{}{15}\ \frac{}{18}$.

4. We live in the state of $\frac{}{9}\ \frac{}{14}\ \frac{}{4}\ \frac{}{9}\ \frac{}{1}\ \frac{}{14}\ \frac{}{1}$.

5. The capital of our state is
$\frac{}{9}\ \frac{}{14}\ \frac{}{4}\ \frac{}{9}\ \frac{}{1}\ \frac{}{14}\ \frac{}{1}\ \frac{}{16}\ \frac{}{15}\ \frac{}{12}\ \frac{}{9}\ \frac{}{19}$.

I N D I A N A ! ! !

ANSWERS: 1.laws 2.capitol 3.governor 4.Indiana 5.Indianapolis

A Rough Row to Hoe!

The people who first came to Indiana were faced with a lot of hard work to survive in their new home. Many of the first settlers were French fur traders, called *voyageurs*, who built trading posts. These traders gave the local Indians beads, blankets, and whiskey in exchange for beaver and other furs.

Circle the things settlers in Indiana would need.

Buzzing Around Indiana!

1. Indiana was the _____ state to enter the Union.
2. The first people to live in Indiana were _____ Americans.
3. The capital of Indiana is _____.
4. _____ Cave is one of the largest caverns in the United States.
5. The _____ River outlines part of Indiana's western border.
6. _____ was the first capital of Indiana.
7. Hammond, Whiting, East Chicago, and Gary are part of the _____ Region.
8. Indiana's current state constitution is its _____.
9. Tenskwatawa was also known as the Shawnee _____.
10. Indiana's highest point is located in the _____ Plains.

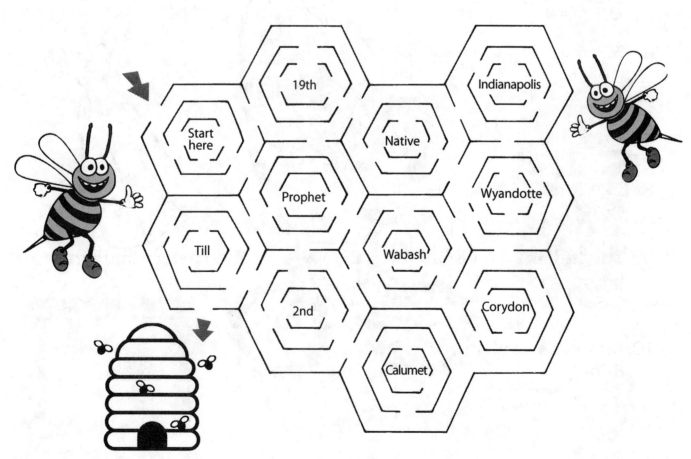

Indiana Through the Years!

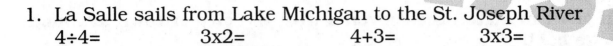

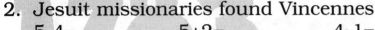

1. La Salle sails from Lake Michigan to the St. Joseph River
   $4÷4=$ $3x2=$ $4+3=$ $3x3=$

2. Jesuit missionaries found Vincennes
   $5-4=$ $5+2=$ $4-1=$ $4÷2=$

3. The Treaty of Paris ends the American Revolution
   $0+1=$ $6+1=$ $4x2=$ $6-3=$

4. Indiana becomes part of the Northwest Territory
   $8÷8=$ $9-2=$ $3+5=$ $1+6=$

5. Indiana becomes the 19th state
   $7-6=$ $7+1=$ $2-1=$ $4+2=$

6. Indianapolis becomes the state capital
   $6÷6=$ $9-1=$ $9-7=$ $7-2=$

7. U.S. Steel plans the city of Gary
   $5÷5=$ $3x3=$ $7-7=$ $5+1=$

8. The first Indianapolis 500 race is held
   $7÷7=$ $4+5=$ $3-2=$ $2-1=$

9. The Indiana Toll Road joins the western and eastern Indiana borders
   $9-8=$ $5+4=$ $3+2=$ $3x2=$

10. Indiana establishes a state lottery
    $8-7=$ $7+2=$ $6+2=$ $1+7=$

ANSWERS: 1.1679 2.1732 3.1783 4.1787 5.1816 6.1825 7.1906 8.1911 9.1956 10.1988

Festive Indiana!

Every year, Indianans have a wide variety of festivals, fairs, and events to choose from.

See if you can match these events with the city or town in which they are held.

1. Parke County Maple Fair

2. Sugar Creek Canoe Race

3. Easter Pageant

4. Tulipfest

5. Glass Festival

6. Miss Indiana Pageant

7. Indiana State Fair

8. Freedom Festival

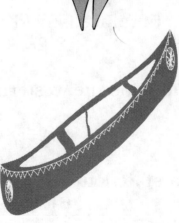

A. Greentown

B. Michigan City

C. Evansville

D. Marion

E. Rockville

F. Crawfordsville

G. Indianapolis

H. Bloomington

ANSWERS: 1.E 2.F 3.D 4.H 5.A 6.B 7.G 8.C

What Did We Do Before Money?

In early Indiana, there were no banks. However, people still wanted to barter, trade, or otherwise "purchase" goods from each other. Wampum, made of shells, bone, or stones, was often swapped for goods. Indians, especially, used wampum for "money." In the barter system, people swapped goods or services. "I'll give you a chicken." "I'll bake you some bread."

Later, banks came into existence, and people began to use money to buy goods. However, they also still bartered when they had no money to spend.

Place a star in the box below the systems used today.

Rhymin' Riddles!

1. I am the Hoosier State, and my name begins with an "I";
    Where the basketballs bounce and the race cars do fly.

    What am I? _____

2. I came to Indiana when I was just a young lad;
    Later I was president, and Civil War made me sad.

    Who am I? _____ _____

3. I am the state rock, made of fossilized shells;
    In Indiana I'm plentiful, and the quarries have done well.

    What am I? _____

4. My brother was the Shawnee Prophet, lost at Tippecanoe;
    I hoped to unite the tribes, into a confederacy that was true.

    Who am I? _____

5. I am the state's own river, so long and so wide;
    Flowing south and west, upon me many canoes did ride.

    What am I? _____ _____

ANSWERS: 1.Indiana 2.Abraham Lincoln 3.limestone 4.Tecumseh 5.Wabash River

 # Map Symbols

Make up symbols for these names and draw them in the space provided on the right.

cave	
dune	
corn	
lake	
chickens	
airport	
fort	
railroad	
hospital	

Indiana Goodies!

Match the name of each crop or product from Indiana with the picture of that item.

corn   apples   tomatoes   eggs

potatoes   tobacco

Indiana's Venomous Snakes!

Several types of snakes live in Indiana, some of which are venomous (poisonous).

Using the alphabet code, see if you can figure out the venomous snakes' names.

A	B	C	D	E	F	G	H	I	J	K	L	M	N	O	P	Q	R	S	T
1	2	3	4	5	6	7	8	9	10	11	12	13	14	15	16	17	18	19	20

U	V	W	X	Y	Z
21	22	23	24	25	26

1. __ __ __ __ __ __ __ __ __ __
   13   1   19   19   1   19   1   21   7   1

2. __ __ __ __ __ __ __ __ __ __
   3   15   16   16   5   18   8   5   1   4

Indiana Battlefields!

Many battles have been fought in Indiana. Some of these were during the Revolutionary War and the Civil War, or were conflicts between settlers and Native Americans.

Using the information given, locate these battle sites on the map of Indiana. Write the year of each battle at its location on the map.

Fort Sackville: In 1779, George Rogers Clark won Fort Sackville, near Vincennes, for a second time from the British.

Portland: In 1791, Chief Little Turtle defeated an army belonging to General Arthur St. Clair, governor of the Northwest Territory, near this location.

Tippecanoe: In 1811, the Shawnee Prophet was defeated by General William Henry Harrison, just north of Lafayette.

Corydon, Salem, and Dupont: In 1863, Confederate General John Hunt Morgan and his Raiders attacked these towns.

Make a Wampum Necklace!

Indiana Native Americans used wampum (beads made from colored shells or stones) to barter with early settlers. They traded wampum for food and supplies. The Indians sometimes traded wampum for trinkets.

You can make your own wampum necklace using dried macaroni and string. Thread the dried macaroni onto a long piece of string and tie.

Wear your necklace to celebrate our state heritage!

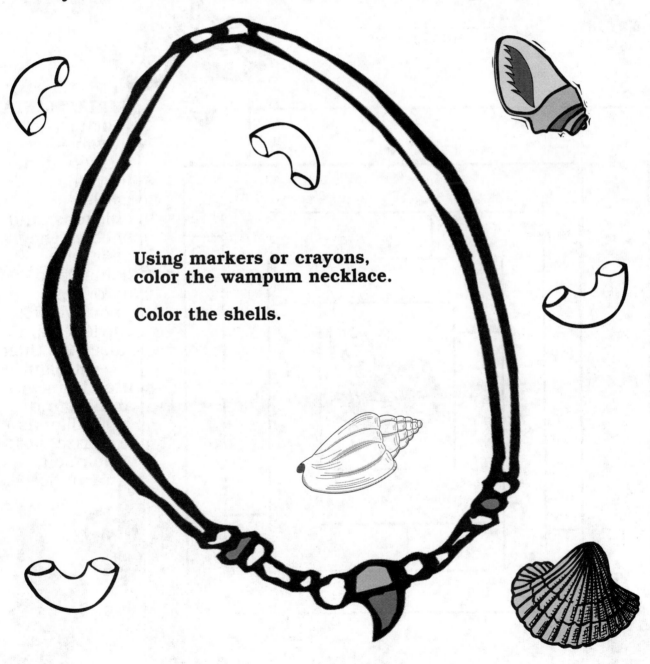

Using markers or crayons, color the wampum necklace.

Color the shells.

Producers and Consumers

Producers (sellers) make goods or provide services. Ralph, a 4th grade student in Corydon, is a consumer because he wants to buy a new wheel for his bicycle.

Help Ralph locate the bicycle-wheel seller so he can fix his bike!

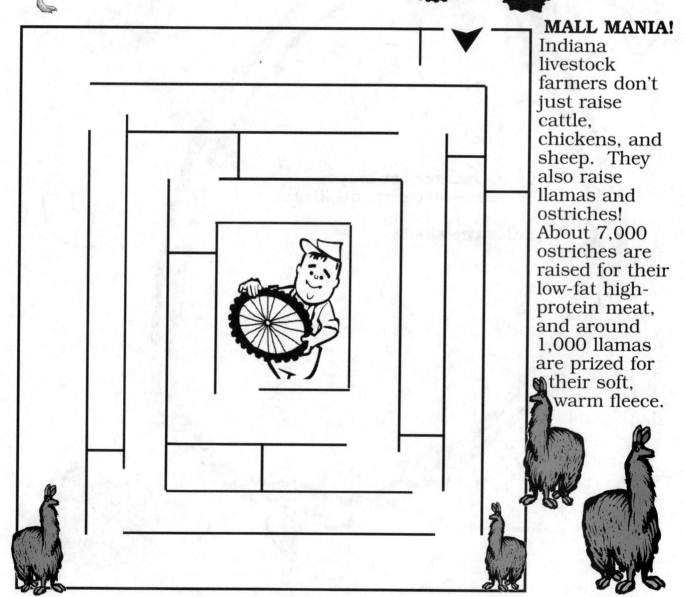

MALL MANIA! Indiana livestock farmers don't just raise cattle, chickens, and sheep. They also raise llamas and ostriches! About 7,000 ostriches are raised for their low-fat high-protein meat, and around 1,000 llamas are prized for their soft, warm fleece.

Indiana Word Wheel!

Use the Word Wheel of Indiana names to complete the sentences below.

1. The earliest known Indiana residents were the _____.
2. The first European known to set foot in Indiana was René-Robert Cavelier, Sieur de _____ _____.
3. The first permanent European settlement in Indiana was

   _____.
4. Indiana was part of the Northwest Territory established by the

   _____ Ordinance in 1787.
5. The last of the Indian Wars took place _____,
   between General Harrison and the Shawnee Prophet.
6. The first capital of Indiana was at _____.
7. Congress' resolution for Indiana statehood was signed by President
   James _____ in 1816.
8. The Harmony Society was founded by a German settler named George

   _____.
9. Central Indiana was taken by the federal government in 1818 as part of
   the _____ _____.
10. In 1863, Confederate General John Hunt _____
    raided southwestern Indiana.

Indiana's Interstates Intersecting!

Indiana's motto is the "Crossroads of America" for more than one reason. Before highways, Indiana's rivers and canals were filled with traffic. The National Road, built in the 1820s, was Indiana's first interstate highway. The National Road was also known as the Cumberland Road. This 600-mile (965-kilometer) road ran from Vandalia, Illinois to Cumberland, Maryland and took thirty years to build! U.S. Route 40 now follows the route of the National Road. Today, more major highways intersect in Indiana than in any other state! So, it's a good idea to learn how to read a road map!

Using the map below to help you, write down the interstate highway (and which direction) you'd take in order to get from.

1. Indianapolis to Terre Haute ___I-70 west___
2. Clarksville to Indianapolis _____
3. Richmond to Indianapolis _____
4. Crawfordsville to Indianapolis _____
5. Greensburg to Shelbyville _____
6. Fort Wayne to Marion _____

Mixed-Up States!

Color, cut out, and paste each of Indiana's four neighbors onto the map below.

Be sure and match the state shapes!

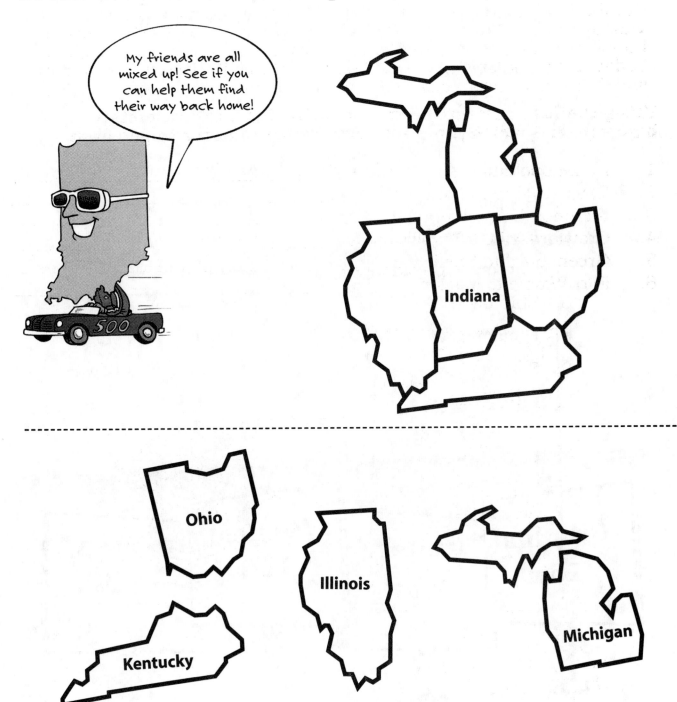

Indiana Law Comes In Many Flavors!

Here is a matching activity for you to see just a few of the many kinds of law it takes to run our state. See how well you do!

People:

1. Bank robber
2. Business person
3. State park ranger
4. Indianans
5. Hospital
6. Real estate agent
7. Corporate president
8. Ship owner
9. Diplomat
10. Soldier

Types of Law:

A. Military Law
B. International Law
C Constitutional Law
D. Medical Law
E. Maritime Law
F. Commercial Law
G. Criminal Law
H. Property Law
I. Antitrust Law
J. Environmental Law

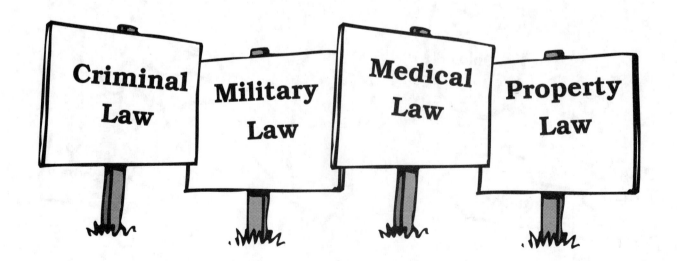

ANSWERS: 1.G 2.F 3.J 4.C 5.D 6.H 7.I 8.E 9.B 10.A

People and Their Jobs!

Can you identify these people and their jobs?

Put an A by the person working on an Indiana farm.
Put a B by the person mining in a south central Indiana limestone quarry.
Put a C by the man unloading freight at Burns Harbor.
Put a D by the photographer from the *Indianapolis Star*.
Put an E by the Indiana railroad engineer.

Watery Highways!

During the early 1800s, Indianans used rivers as their main means of transportation, and canals were built to connect the rivers. Today, the Crossroads of America is served by some of the best waterways in the nation. Lake Michigan is part of the Great Lakes St. Lawrence Seaway that allows ships to travel between the Great Lakes and the Atlantic Ocean. Several ports on Lake Michigan service Indiana, including Indiana Harbor and Burns Waterway Harbor. Much of the freight handled at these ports is headed for factories in the Calumet region of Indiana. Canals link the ports with the Illinois Waterway, which connects with the Mississippi River. The Ohio River is the main waterway in southern Indiana, and river barges travel up and down to the many ports in the area.

When you're on board a ship, you have to use special terms to talk about directions. Label the ships below with these terms:

bow: front of the ship
stern: back of the ship
fore: towards the bow
aft: towards the stern
port: left as you face the bow
starboard: right as you face the bow

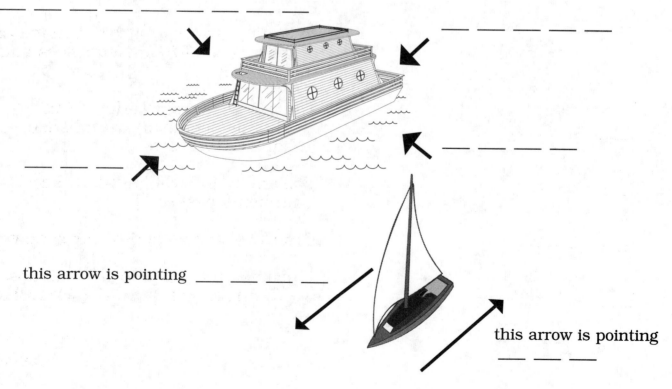

this arrow is pointing ___ ___ ___ ___

this arrow is pointing ___ ___ ___

Politics As Usual

Our elected government officials decide how much money is going to be spent on schools, roads, public parks, and libraries. It's very important for the citizens of the state to understand what's going on in their government and how it will affect them. Below are some political words that are often used when talking about government.

MATCH EACH POLITICAL WORD WITH ITS DEFINITION.

_____ 1. Constitution

_____ 2. Governor

_____ 3. Chief Justice

_____ 4. General Assembly

_____ 5. District

_____ 6. Amendment

_____ 7. Term

_____ 8. Election

_____ 9. Veto

_____ 10. Bill

A. Number of years that an official is elected to serve

B. Lead Judge on the State Supreme Court

C. The chief executive

D. An addition to the Constitution

E. The selection, by vote, of a candidate for office

F. Indiana's law-making body, made up of the House of Representatives and the Senate

G. The present version adopted in 1851, this document established Indiana's state laws

H. The ability to forbid a bill or law from being passed

I. Draft of a law presented for review

J. A division of a state for the purpose of electing a representative from that division

ANSWERS: 1.G 2.C 3.B 4.F 5.J 6.D 7.A 8.E 9.H 10.I

What Shall I Be When I Grow Up?

Here are just a few of the jobs that kept early Indianans busy.

Lawyer	Prospector	Silversmith
Judge	Woodcarver	Cabinetmaker
Politician	Housekeeper	Carpenter
Teacher	Dairyman	Gardener
Mayor	Servant	Cook
Weaver	Cooper (barrelmaker)	Laundress
Mantuamaker (dressmaker)	Barber	Stablehand
Musician	Printer	Baker
Jeweler	Bookbinder	Fisherman
Tailor	Innkeeper	Milliner (hatmaker)
Pharmacist	Minister	Blacksmith
Doctor	Gaoler (jailer)	Gunsmith
Soldier	Governor	Hunter

You are a young settler trying to decide what you want to be when you grow up.

Choose a career and next to it write a description of what you think you would do each day as a:

Write your career choice here!

_____   _____

_____

Write your career choice here!

_____   _____

_____

Write your career choice here!

_____   _____

_____

Write your career choice here!

_____   _____

_____

Create Your Own Quarter!

Look at the change in your pocket. You might notice that one of the coins has changed. The United States is minting new quarters, one for each of the fifty states. Each quarter has a design on it that says something special about one particular state. Indiana will have its very own state quarter in 2002!

What if you had designed the Indiana quarter? Draw a picture of how you would like the Indiana quarter to look. Make sure you include things that are special about Indiana.

Indiana's Governor!

The governor is the leader of the state.

Do some research to complete this biography of the governor.

Governor's name:

_____

Paste a picture of the governor here: ▶

The governor was born in this state:

_____

The governor was born on this date:

_____

Members of the governor's family:

_____

_____

Interesting facts about the governor:

_____

_____

_____

_____

_____

The ORIGINAL Indianans!

The Indian tribes of the state of Indiana included the Miami, Potawatomi, Delaware, Kickapoo, and Shawnee. Many of these early tribes arrived from the eastern states because they were being pushed off their land there. Most tribes only stayed in the Indiana territory for 25 to 50 years before moving further west. The Miami Indian tribe established the most permanent roots in Indiana, living in the state for almost 150 years. They lived in the New World before the explorers and settlers came.

Circle the things that Native Americans might have used in their everyday life.

States All Around Code-Buster!

Decipher the code and write in the names of the states that border Indiana.

A B C D E F G H I J K L M N O P Q R

S T U V W X Y Z

---

1. ___ ___ ___ ___ ___ ___ ___ ___ ___

2. ___ ___ ___ ___ ___ ___ ___ ___ ___

3. ___ ___ ___ ___ ___ ___ ___ ___ ___

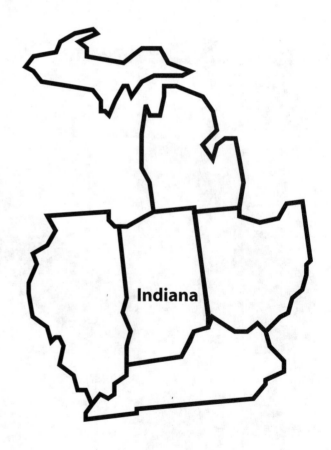

Indiana

4. ___ ___ ___ ___

Incomparable Indiana Place Names!

Can you figure out the compound words that make up the names of these Indiana places?

_____ _____
AMBOY

_____ _____
CENTERPOINT

_____ _____
GOLDSMITH

_____ _____
ATWOOD

_____ _____
CHARLESTOWN

_____ _____
GRANDVIEW

_____ _____
BEDFORD

_____ _____
DONALDSON

_____ _____
GREENFIELD

_____ _____
BIRDSEYE

_____ _____
EDWARDSPORT

_____ _____
KINGMAN

_____ _____
BUCKSKIN

_____ _____
FAIRLAND

_____ _____
NEWBERRY

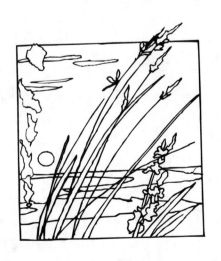

Looking For a Home!

Draw a line from the things on the left to their homes on the right!

1. Indiana's governor

2. Studebakers

3. the horse-drawn canal boat *Ben Franklin*

4. military history buffs

5. heavy reader

6. hikers and horseback riders

7. Honest Abe fan

8. exotic butterflies and other animals

9. Amish farmers

10. spelunkers

A. the Indiana Military Museum

B. Lincoln Boyhood National Memorial

C. Mesker Park Zoo and Botanic Garden

D. Wyandotte Cave

E. Whitewater Canal State Historic Site

F. Studebaker National Museum

G. Indianapolis

H. Brown County State Park

I. Elkhart and Lagrange counties

J. the Lilly Library at Indiana University

ANSWERS: 1.G 2.F 3.E 4.A 5.J 6.H 7.B 8.C 9.I 10.D

Weather to Please!

Indianans experience all four seasons during the year. Winter is usually a time of snow. Northern Indiana, near Lake Michigan, receives a lot of "lake effect" snow, as much as 100 inches (254 centimeters) a year, but the lake keeps temperatures milder than would be expected. Spring is tornado season all over the Midwest, and Indiana is no exception. Spring rains can also cause the Ohio River to flood. Southern Indiana often has late summer droughts, but the area has a longer growing season than the northern part of the state. Autumn is a beautiful time, and the forests and woodlands are bright with the colors of the changing leaves.

The highest temperature ever recorded was 116°F (47°C) in 1936, but the average July temperature is usually around 75°F (24°C). The coldest Indiana temperature was recorded in 1951, when it dropped to -35°F (-37°C)! Usually, winter temperatures in January are around 28°F (-2°C).

On the thermometer gauges below, color the mercury red (°F) to show the hottest temperature ever recorded in Indiana. Color the mercury blue (°F) to show the coldest temperature ever recorded in Indiana.

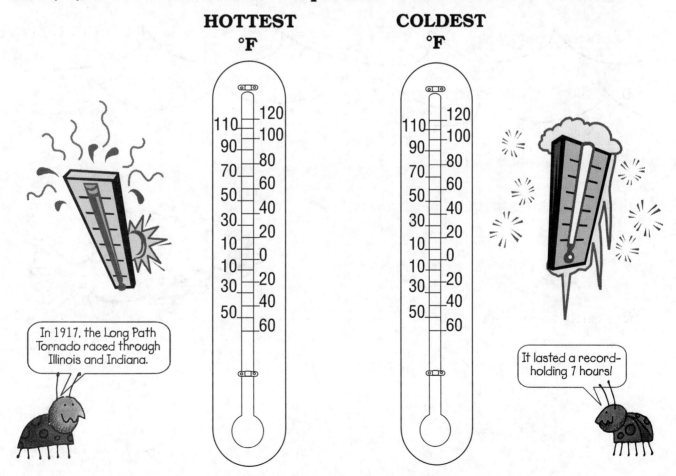

HOTTEST °F   COLDEST °F

In 1917, the Long Path Tornado raced through Illinois and Indiana.

It lasted a record-holding 7 hours!

Something Fishy Here!

Indiana has many rivers and lakes. Most of the rivers in Indiana flow southward and westward into the Mississippi River system. The Wabash River, which is about 500 miles (800 kilometers) long, outlines part of Indiana's western border and pours into the Ohio River. In fact, many of the other rivers in Indiana are tributaries of the Wabash River.

Indiana has around 1,000 small natural lakes, most of which are in the northern part of the state. Lake Wawasee is Indiana's largest natural lake, and covers almost 5 square miles (13 square kilometers)! Many of Indiana's other natural lakes are called kettle lakes, and were created thousands of years ago by glaciers. In the central part of the state, many of the smaller streams have been dammed up to create several artificial lakes.

Draw what is going on above the water line (a boat, fishermen) and add some other underwater fish friends.

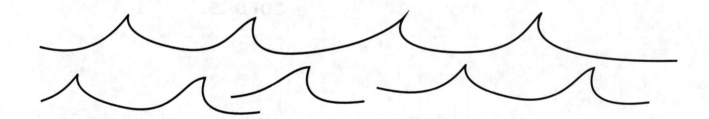

The Scenic Route

Imagine that you are the official tour guide for your class and you're taking your classmates on a trip to some famous Indiana places.

Circle these sites and cities on the map below, then number them in the order you would visit if you were traveling north to south through the state:

____ Terre Haute   ____ Lake Michigan

____ Gary   ____ Wabash River

____ Evansville   ____ Indianapolis

____ Tippecanoe River   ____ Bloomington

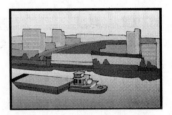

Map labels: Lake Michigan, Gary, Valparaiso, South Bend, St. Joseph River, Waterloo, Tippecanoe River, Fort Wayne, Logansport, Wabash, Wabash River, Lafayette, Portland, Rileysburg, Muncie, Indianapolis, Terre Haute, Bloomington, Columbus, Seymour, Dupont, Vincennes, Salem, Corydon, Evansville

Key to a Map!

A map key, also called a map legend, shows symbols which represent different things on a map.

Match each word with a symbol for things found in the state of Indiana.

airport

church

cave

railroad

river

road

school

state capital

battle site

bird sanctuary

Brother, Can You Spare a Dime?

After the collapse of the stock market on Wall Street in 1929, the state of Indiana, along with the rest of the nation, plunged headfirst into the Great Depression. It was the worst economic crisis America had ever known. Banks closed and businesses crashed...there was financial ruin everywhere. Thousands of Indianans lost their jobs, and many of the coal mines and stone quarries in southern Indiana closed down.

Our President Helps

While the nation was in the midst of the Depression, Franklin Delano Roosevelt became president. With America on the brink of economic devastation, the federal government stepped forward and hired unemployed people to build parks, bridges, and roads. With this help, and other government assistance, the country began to slowly, and painfully, pull out of the Great Depression. Within the first 100 days of his office, Roosevelt enacted a number of policies to help minimize the suffering of the nation's many unemployed workers. These programs were known as the NEW DEAL. The jobs helped families support themselves and improved the country's infrastructure.

Put an X next to the jobs that were part of Roosevelt's New Deal.

1. computer programmer _____

2. bridge builder _____

3. fashion model _____

4. park builder _____

5. interior designer _____

6. hospital builder _____

7. school builder _____

8. website designer _____

ANSWERS: 2 4 6 7

The First Americans

When European explorers first arrived in America, they found many American Indian tribes living in Indiana.

Shawnee Indians lived in Indiana in the Eastern Woodlands region of the United States. The types of homes they lived in were wigwams. **Color the Eastern Woodlands green.**

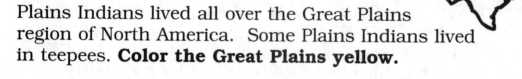

Plains Indians lived all over the Great Plains region of North America. Some Plains Indians lived in teepees. **Color the Great Plains yellow.**

Pueblo Indians lived in the Southwest region of North America. They lived in multi-story terraced buildings, called pueblos. **Color the Southwest red.**

The Five Civilized Tribes and other Indians lived in the Southeast region of the United States. They lived in rectangular thatched houses called wattle and daub. **Color the Southeast blue.**

Color these houses Indians lived in. Then draw a line from the type of house to the correct region.

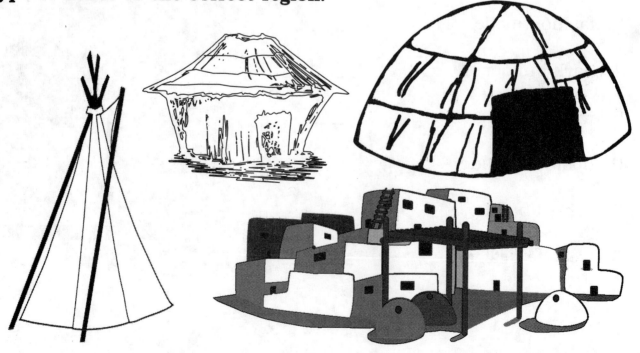

Indiana Immigration

People have come to Indiana from many other states and countries. As time has gone by, Indiana's population has grown more diverse. This means that people of different races and from different cultures and ethnic backgrounds have moved to Indiana.

Many of Indiana's early settlers were descended from English, Welsh, and Scottish people. Many immigrants also came to the state from Germany, Ireland, Poland, Hungary, Belgium, and Italy. In the early 1800s, Quakers, Amish, and Mennonites settled in various places around Indiana. More recently, people have come to the state from Mexico, Canada, Great Britain, and Southeast Asia. Only a certain number of immigrants are allowed to move to America each year. Many of these immigrants eventually become U.S. citizens.

**Read the statement and decide if it's a fact or an opinion.
Write your answer on the line.**

1. Many of Indiana's early immigrants came from Europe. _____

2. Lots of immigrants speak a language other than English. _____

3. The clothing immigrants wear is very interesting. _____

4. Immigrants from England have a neat accent when
they speak. _____

5. Many immigrants will become United States citizens. _____

6. Many recent immigrants come from Canada and
Southeast Asia. _____

An immigrant is a person who migrates to another country in hopes of a better life.

ANSWERS: 1.Fact 2.Fact 3.Opinion 4.Opinion 5.Fact 6.Fact

A Day in the Life of a Pioneer!

**Pretend you are a settler in the days of early Indiana.
You keep a diary of what you do each day.
Write in the "diary" what you might have done
on a long, hot summer day in July 1734.**

This Old House!

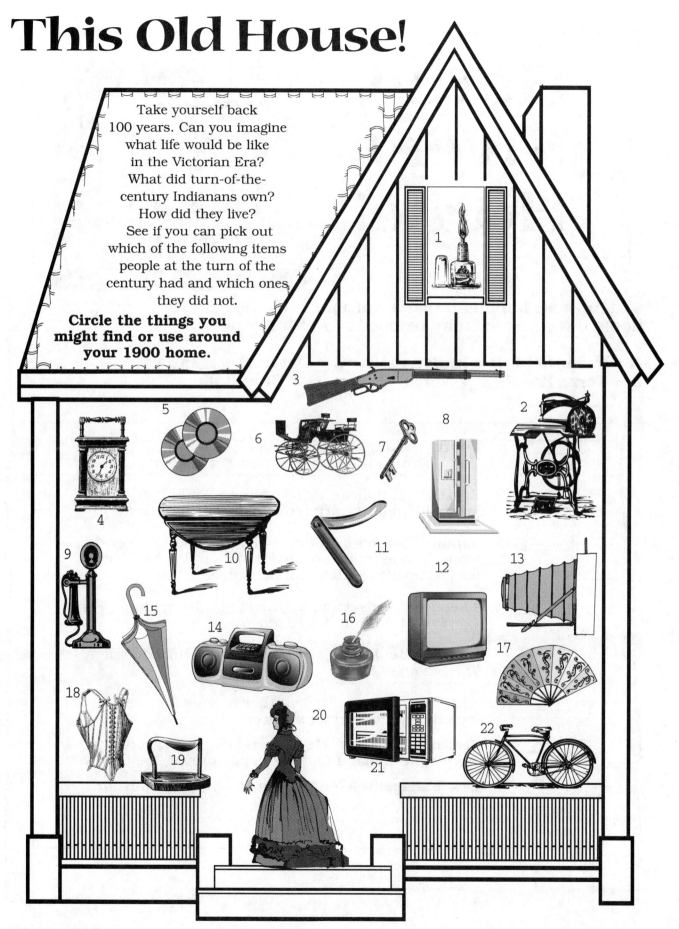

Take yourself back 100 years. Can you imagine what life would be like in the Victorian Era? What did turn-of-the-century Indianans own? How did they live? See if you can pick out which of the following items people at the turn of the century had and which ones they did not.

Circle the things you might find or use around your 1900 home.

Home, Sweet Home!

Match these famous Indiana authors with their native or adopted hometowns. Some may be used more than once.

**A = Greenfield B = Indianapolis C = Dana D = Kentland
E = Terre Haute F = North Vernon G = Brookville**

_____ 1. **Booth Tarkington:** Pulitzer Prize-winning author of *The Magnificent Ambersons* and *Alice Adams*.

_____ 2. **Ernie Pyle:** Pulitzer Prize-winning World War II journalist, killed during the Okinawa campaign.

_____ 3. **James Whitcomb Riley:** called the Hoosier Poet, he wrote for the *Indianapolis Journal*, and is best known for poems like "Little Orphan Annie."

_____ 4. **Theodore Dreiser:** wrote tragic novels including *Sister Carrie* and *An American Tragedy*.

_____ 5. **George Ade**: humorist who wrote the comedy opera *The Sultan of Sulu.*

_____ 6. **Kurt Vonnegut:** offbeat author of several novels including *Slaughterhouse Five.*

_____ 7. **Jessamyn West:** wrote *The Friendly Persuasion*, the story of an Indiana Quaker family during the Civil War.

_____ 8. **Lew Wallace:** soldier and author; most famous for *Ben-Hur.*

ANSWERS: 1.B 2.C 3.A 4.E 5.D 6.B 7.F 8.G

Indiana Spelling Bee!

Good spelling is a good habit. Study the words on the left side of the page. Then fold the page in half and "take a spelling test" on the right side. Have a buddy read the words aloud to you. When done, unfold the page and check your spelling. Keep your score. **GOOD LUCK.**

Amish _____

Bloomington _____

Calumet _____

communications _____

Evansville _____

geography _____

glacier _____

Hoosier _____

Indianapolis _____

Kickapoo _____

Lincoln _____

Mennonite _____

pioneer _____

Quaker _____

railroad _____

Vincennes _____

Wabash _____

Indiana Women and the Vote!

Before the 19th Amendment to the United States Constitution, women were unable to vote in the United States. In 1919, women gained suffrage in Indiana and began voting for the first time. In 1920, enough states ratified the amendment and it became the law of the land. Women gained total suffrage nationally. Women today continue to be a major force in the election process.

Match the words in the left box with their definitions in the right box.

1. Amendment _____	A. The right to vote
2. Ratify _____	B. A law that is an acceptable practice throughout the nation
3. Constitution _____	C. People who could not vote in Indiana until 1919
4. State Senate _____	D. An addition to the U.S. Constitution
5. Law of the Land _____	E. The selection, by vote, of a candidate for office
6. Election _____	F. To give approval
7. Suffrage _____	G. The fundamental law of the United States that was framed in 1787 and put into effect in 1789
8. Women _____	H. One-half of the legislature in the state of Indiana

ANSWERS: 1.D 2.F 3.G 4.H 5.B 6.E 7.A 8.C

Indiana's Crossroads Commodities!

Fill in the bubblegram with the names of the state's natural resources. Use the first and last letters as your clues.

WORD BANK

WHEAT
FRUIT
LIMESTONE
CORN
OATS
COAL

1. ◯ ◯ __ L

2. C ◯ __ ◯

3. ◯ __ __ __ ◯ __ __ __ S

4. O ◯ __ ◯

5. L ◯ __ __ __ __ __ ◯ __

6. __ ◯ __ __ T

7. W __ ◯ __ __

Now unscramble the "bubble" letters to find out the mystery word!
HINT: What is one way we can help to save our environment?

__ __ __ __ __ __ __ __ __ __ __ __

Can you Dig It?

Indiana is the ninth leading producer of coal in the United States. Most of the bituminous coal is mined from an enormous coalfield that is underneath western and southwestern Indiana. Indiana coal is high in sulfur, which can pollute the air when the coal is burned. Quarries in south-central Indiana supplied the limestone for the Empire State Building in New York City and the Pentagon in Washington, D.C.! Other minerals found in Indiana include stone, cement, sand, gravel, petroleum, clays, gypsum, and lime.

Put the names of these minerals found in Indiana in alphabetical order, by numbering them 1 to 10.

_____ gypsum

_____ limestone

_____ sulfur

_____ bituminous

_____ sand

_____ clay

_____ gravel

_____ cement

_____ lime

_____ petroleum

ANSWERS: 1.bituminous 2.cement 3.clay 4.gravel 5.gypsum 6.lime 7.limestone 8.petroleum 9.sand 10.sulfur

You've Got Mail!

Send an e-mail to the past. E-mail a boy or girl from early Indiana and tell them what they are missing in today's world.

WRITE   SAVE   SEND   DELETE   INTERNET
                                       NEWS AND NOTES

Who knows? You may even get a message in return... a message written on parchment with a quill pen telling you what you are missing from a simpler time!

The gas mask that World War I and World War II soldiers used was invented by James B. Garner of Lebanon in 1915!

What a Great Idea!

These are just some of the amazing Indiana inventions and inventors.

WORD BANK

plow
perfume
automobile
gasoline
beans

1. Sylvanus F. Bowser of Fort Wayne developed the first practical
   _ _ _ _ _ _ _ _ pump in 1885. He got a patent for his
   invention in 1887.

2. Elwood Haynes of Kokomo developed the first gas-powered clutch-
   driven _ _ _ _ _ _ _ _ _ _ _ in the 1890s. Haynes also
   invented a type of stainless steel in 1906 when he was working on
   tarnish-free silverware for his wife!

3. In 1857, James Oliver of South Bend got a patent for his hardened
   steel _ _ _ _ that was more efficient than older models. He
   became a multimillionaire with his "plow that broke the plains."

4. Indianapolis grocer Gilbert Van Camp created a food found at
   cookouts across America when he sold his family recipe of pork and
   _ _ _ _ _ _. Now it's a favorite at cookouts across the country!

5. Sarah Walker of Indianapolis built a factory to produce cosmetics
   and _ _ _ _ _ _ _, and changed her name to Madame C.J.
   Walker. She became one of the nation's first woman millionaires!

ANSWERS: 1.gasoline 2.automobile 3.plow 4.beans 5.perfume

Headlining Hoosier Scavenger Hunt!

Here is a list of some of the famous people associated with Indiana. **Go on a scavenger hunt to see if you can "capture" a fact about each one. Use an encyclopedia, almanac, or other resource you might need. Happy hunting!**

FAMOUS PERSON	FAMOUS FACT
Hoagland (Hoagy) Carmichael	_____
Edward Eggleston	_____
Benjamin Harrison	_____
William Henry Harrison	_____
James Hoffa	_____
Robert Knight	_____
David Letterman	_____
Thomas Riley Marshall	_____
Caleb Mills	_____
Meredith Nicholson	_____
James Oliver	_____
Jane Pauley	_____
Gene Stratton Porter	_____
James Danforth Quayle	_____
James Whitcomb Riley	_____
Twyla Tharp	_____
Kurt Vonnegut	_____
Wendell Willkie	_____
Wilbur Wright	_____

Johnny Appleseed

WORD BANK
apple
walked
Chapman
folk
Indiana

Use the words from the Word Bank to fill in the blanks in the story below. Some words may be used more than once.

During the 19th century, a man named John _ _ _ _ _ _ _ took up an interesting profession. He _ _ _ _ _ _ all over the area where Ohio, Illinois, and _ _ _ _ _ _ _ are today. As he _ _ _ _ _ _, he planted _ _ _ _ _ seeds. Because of his habit, he became known as Johnny _ _ _ _ _seed.

Johnny became well known as a _ _ _ _ hero, recognized in every log cabin from the Ohio River to the Great Lakes. For more than 40 years, he travelled and planted _ _ _ _ _ trees. Finally, in the summer of 1847 he came to the house of a settler in Allen County, _ _ _ _ _ _ _. He was warmly welcomed, ate some bread and milk, and talked with the family. Johnny _ _ _ _ _seed spent the last night of his 72-year life there with the family. Johnny continues to be an important _ _ _ _ hero, and his legacy of beautiful _ _ _ _ _ trees continue to remind us of him to this day.

Map of North America

This is a map of North America. Indiana is one of the 50 states.

Color the state of Indiana red.

Color the rest of the United States yellow. Alaska and Hawaii are part of the United States and should also be colored yellow.

Color Canada green. Color Mexico blue.

The Indiana Amish and Mennonites

Amish and Mennonite people have been living in Indiana since the 1800s. The Amish began as a branch of the Mennonite faith. A Swiss Mennonite bishop named Jakob Amman formed his own group, the Amish, in 1693. Both the Mennonites and the Amish lived peaceful lives, and condemned violence. Unfortunately, at that time all Mennonites were being persecuted in Europe. Many of the Mennonites and Amish fled to America to start a new life, and many of them settled in Indiana. Today, the Mennonite church at Berne has one of the largest Mennonite groups in the United States.

The Amish settled in Elkhart, Lagrange, and Daviess counties. According to the Amish *ordnung*, or rules, they are forbidden to drive cars, use electricity, or go to public places of entertainment like movie theaters. They are known for their style of dress, which is plain and simple. Women wear black dresses, bonnets, and shawls, and the men traditionally wear hats and don't trim their beards. They live mostly by farming, and are often seen driving horse-drawn buggies.

Read each statement about the Amish and Mennonites, and decide if it's true (T) or false (F).

1. The Mennonites live very violent lives. ____

2. The Amish are farmers. ____

3. The Amish are named after Jakob Amman. ____

4. The Amish do not use electricity or cars. ____

5. Amish men are clean-shaven. ____

6. The Mennonites were treated well in Europe. ____

ANSWERS: 1.F 2.T 3.T 4.T 5.F 6.F

The Hoosier State!

Color the state of Indiana. What color? Yellow like ripe corn, of course! Circle the state capital.

Lake Michigan

South Bend

Waterloo

Valparaiso

Columbia City

Fort Wayne

Huntington

Kent-land

Logansport

Wabash

Decatur

Marion

Kokomo

Portland

Lafayette

Dayton

Muncie

Rileysburg

Richmond

Indianapolis

Shelbyville

Terre Haute

Batesville

Bloomington

Columbus

Greendale

Seymour

Bedford

Madison

Washington

Vincennes

Salem

New Albany

Evansville

20

Indiana State Greats!

How many of these state greats from the great state of Indiana do you know?

Use an encyclopedia, almanac, or other resource to match the following facts with the state great they describe.

Hint: There are 2 facts for each state great!

1. NASA astronaut

2. professional basketball player; considered one of the all-time greats

3. vice-president of the United States under George Bush

4. flew on the second American spaceflight; made the first two-man spaceflight with John Young in 1965

5. won a record seven gold medals in the 1972 Olympic Games

6. dancer and choreographer

7. played for the Boston Celtics and coached the Indiana Pacers

8. represented Indiana in the U.S. House of Representatives from 1977 to 1981

9. Olympic swimmer

10. composes dances that combine classical ballet, tap dance, and popular social dances

A. Larry Bird

B. Virgil "Gus" Grissom

C. Twyla Tharp

D. Mark Spitz

E. James Danforth Quayle

ANSWERS: 1.B 2.A 3.E 4.B 5.D 6.C 7.A 8.E 9.D 10.C

Indiana Writers!

Fill in the missing first or last name of these famous Indiana writers.

1. First name: Rex
   Last name: _____

2. First name: _____
   Last name: Porter

3. First name: Booth
   Last name: _____

4. First name: _____
   Last name: Dreiser

5. First name: Ernie
   Last name: _____

6. First name: _____
   Last name: Nicholson

7. First name: James Maurice
   Last name: _____

8. First name: Eggleston
   Last name: _____

9. First name: Jessamyn
   Last name: _____

9. First name: _____
   Last name: Ward

To be a reader or not to be a reader — there's only one answer!

ANSWERS: 1.Stout 2.Gene Stratton 3.Tarkington 4.Theodore 5.Pyle 6.Meredith 7.Thompson 8.Edward 9.West 10.Mary Jane

Virtual Indiana!

Using your knowledge of Indiana, make a website that explains different places in Indiana. You can even draw pictures of animals, places, people, and other fun stuff, to make your very own interesting website.

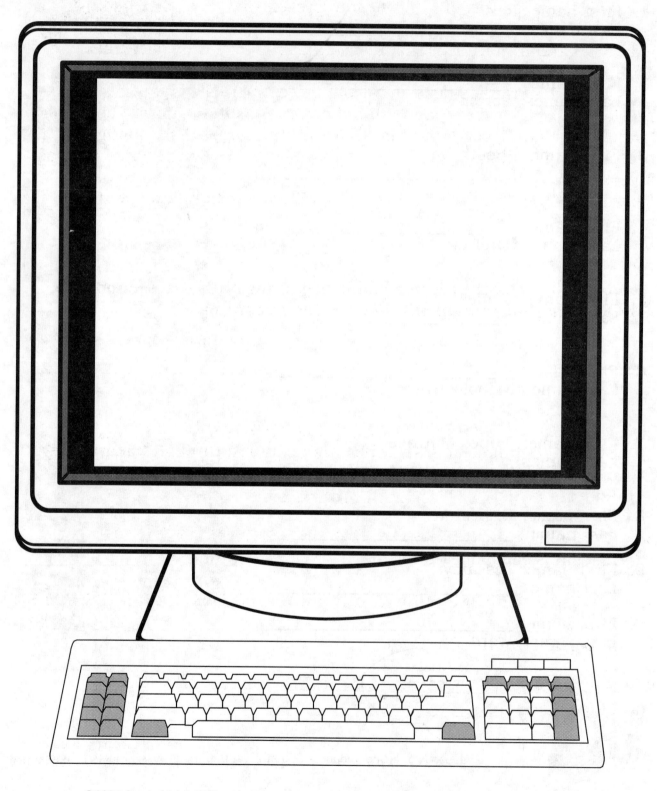

Honest Abe!

One of Indiana's most famous residents didn't even move there until he was eight years old! Abraham Lincoln was born on February 12, 1806 in Kentucky. In December of 1816, his family travelled northwest, across the Ohio River, into present-day Spencer County. They settled near Pigeon Creek, where Abraham's father Thomas built a cabin. Abraham lived in Indiana until he was 21 years old.

Most historians consider Lincoln to be America's greatest president. His speeches made him a national political figure. Lincoln's "House Divided" speech and his "Gettysburg Address" are among his best remembered, and people quote those speeches to this day. He was a perfect example of how much the "self-educated" man can achieve. He was a pioneer in civil rights with his Emancipation Proclamation, and he took the first step toward ending the injustice of slavery. Even today, Lincoln is still revered as an honest and ethical man and a true American hero!

Cross out every other letter below beginning with the second one. The letters that remain will answer the questions.

1. H H O L U B S T E M D E I T V M I T D R E B D L
    In a famous speech Lincoln said a "_ _ _ _ _ _ _ _ _ _ _ _ _ against itself cannot stand."

2. T R W M O P M L I G N F U R T Z E T S A
    Even though Lincoln's speeches have endured through history, they did not necessarily take him a long time to say. His Gettysburg Address lasted _ _ _ _ _ _ _ _ _ _.

3. E C T B H R I T C L S M H M O T N R E Z S X T B Y B
    Lincoln is remembered for his _ _ _ _ _ _ and _ _ _ _ _ _ _.

4. G L E R T A T X Y C S T B G U B R C G A G D B D A R B E R S M S T
    Lincoln's _ _ _ _ _ _ _ _ _ _ _ _ _ _ _ _ _ _ _ outlined the importance of the Civil War.

5. S A E C L B F X E L D G U R C D A B T M E O D Q
    Lincoln was a _ _ _ _-_ _ _ _ _ _ _ _ _ man.

A River Runs Through It!

The state of Indiana is blessed with many rivers. See if you can wade right in and figure out which river name completes the sentences below!

1. In the Land of Opposites, the name of the __ __ __ __ __ River would be the "Black River."

2. The __ __ __ __ __ __ River forms part of the western border of the state before it cuts across the center of Indiana.

3. The __ __ __ __ River forms the southern border of the state.

4. The __ __ __ __ __ __ __ __ __ __ River was the site of a battle between General Harrison and the Shawnee Prophet.

5. I wonder if the __ __ __ River is filled with swimming snakes?

6. The __ __ __ __ __ __ River can be found both in eastern Indiana and in western Ohio.

RIVER BANK

Wabash	Eel
Maumee	White
Tippecanoe	Ohio

ANSWERS: 1.White 2.Wabash 3.Ohio 4.Tippecanoe 5.Eel 6.Maumee

Indiana Trivia!

I ♥ Indiana!

NO FUZZY KISSES!
In Indiana, it is illegal to have a mustache if you kiss other people all the time!

RAGGEDY ANN'S MOM!
Marcella Gruelle of Indianapolis created the Raggedy Ann doll in 1914.

HO! HO! HO!
Every year, Santa Claus, Indiana receives more than 500,000 letters asking for Christmas presents.

SHOT HEARD 'ROUND THE WORLD!
On October 22, 1917, Sergeant Alexander Arch of South Bend became the first American to fire a shot in World War I.

WHERE'D THEY GO?
Although "Indiana" means "land of the Indians," only about 8,000 Native Americans actually live in the state.

DO THEY MEASURE UP?
In Indiana, hotel sheets must be exactly 99 inches (251.5 centimeters) long and 81 inches (205.7 centimeters) wide.

DRAGON BREATH!
In Gary, it is illegal for someone to go to a movie house, theater, or ride a public streetcar within four hours of eating garlic.

DRIVE-IN FUN!
In the 1920s, Shelby County became the home of the first drive-in movie theater!

Now write down another fact that you know about Indiana.

_____

_____

Independence Day

We celebrate America's birthday on July 4. We call the 4th of July Independence Day because this is the day America declared its independence from England.

Circle the things you might enjoy on this special holiday.

Pretend you are signing the Declaration of Independence.

Write your signature here. You can even make it fancy!

Declaration of Independence

_____

Indiana Twisters!

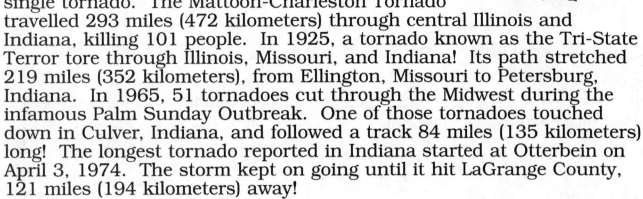

In the spring, the Midwest is threatened by tornadoes, and several touch down in Indiana each year. In 1917, Indiana was part of the longest continuous track ever recorded for a single tornado. The Mattoon-Charleston Tornado travelled 293 miles (472 kilometers) through central Illinois and Indiana, killing 101 people. In 1925, a tornado known as the Tri-State Terror tore through Illinois, Missouri, and Indiana! Its path stretched 219 miles (352 kilometers), from Ellington, Missouri to Petersburg, Indiana. In 1965, 51 tornadoes cut through the Midwest during the infamous Palm Sunday Outbreak. One of those tornadoes touched down in Culver, Indiana, and followed a track 84 miles (135 kilometers) long! The longest tornado reported in Indiana started at Otterbein on April 3, 1974. The storm kept on going until it hit LaGrange County, 121 miles (194 kilometers) away!

Using the information in the paragraphs above, graph the lengths (in miles) of the tracks left by these tornadoes. The first one has been done for you.

- Tri-State Terror (1925)
- Culver, Indiana (1965)
- Mattoon-Charleston (1917)
- LaGrange (1974)

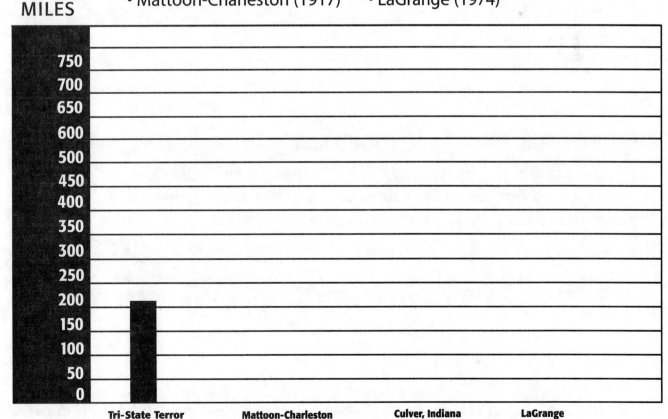

Indiana Gazetteer!

A gazetteer is a list of places. Use the word bank to complete the names of some of these famous places in our state.

1. The George Rogers __ __ __ __ __ National Historical Park, in Vincennes
2. __ __ __ __ __ __ __ __ __ Cave, near Leavenworth
3. The Indianapolis Motor __ __ __ __ __ __ __ __, in Indianapolis
4. The home of James Whitcomb __ __ __ __ __, in Greenfield
5. The Indiana __ __ __ __ __ National Lakeshore
6. The Indianapolis Museum of __ __ __
7. The Indiana Repertory __ __ __ __ __ __ __, in Indianapolis
8. The Old __ __ __ __ __ __ __ __ __ Library in Vincennes

WORD BANK

Art	Riley	Speedway	Clark
Theater	Wyandotte	Cathedral	Dunes

A Hoosier Hodgepodge!

Unscramble the words below to get the scoop on these Indiana state facts.

1. ONEPY   _____   STATE FLOWER

2. NIRALCDA   _____   STATE BIRD

3. PULTI ERTE   _____   STATE TREE

4. ODARSSSOCR
   FO MERICAA   _____   STATE MOTTO

5. SIEROHO TSTAE   _____   STATE NICKNAME

6. SAWHAB VERIR   _____   STATE RIVER

Industrious Indiana!

Indiana has a diverse economy that includes many different industries. Some industries in the state include manufacturing, farming, and tourism. Agriculture is very important in the state, with more than 60,000 farms. Hoosiers raise a variety of crops and livestock. Indiana is the 9th biggest producer of coal in the country! Manufacturing is also big in the state, especially in the heavily industrial Calumet region. Indiana manufacturers produce paper products, automobile parts, clothing, textiles, printed materials, electronics, and many, many other things!

Complete these sentences.

Without refrigeration units, I couldn't _____

_____

Without electricity, I couldn't _____

_____

Without agriculture, I couldn't _____

_____

Without coal, I couldn't _____

_____

Without tourism, I couldn't _____

_____

Without machinery, I couldn't _____

_____

Pioneer Corn Husk Doll

You can make a corn husk doll similar to the dolls
Indiana settlers' children played with! Here's how:

You will need:
- corn husks (or strips of cloth)
- string
- scissors

1. **Select a long piece of corn husk and fold
   it in half. Tie a string about one inch
   (2.54 centimeters) down from the fold to
   make the doll's head.**

2. **Roll a husk and put it between the layers of the tied husk,
   next to the string. Tie another string around the longer
   husk, just below the rolled husk. Now your doll has arms!
   Tie short pieces of string at the ends of the rolled husk to
   make the doll's hands.**

3. **Make your doll's waist by tying another string around the
   longer husk.**

4. **If you want your doll to have legs, cut the longer husk up
   the middle. Tie the two halves at the bottom to
   make feet.**

5. **Add eyes and a nose to your doll with a marker. You could
   use corn silk for the doll's hair.**

**Now you can
make a whole
family of dolls!**

Indiana Timeline!

A timeline is a list of important events and the year that they happened. You can use a timeline to understand more about history. Read the timeline about Indiana history, then see if you can answer the questions at the bottom.

1679..........René-Robert Cavelier, Sieur de La Salle, sails into the St. Joseph River

1732..........Jesuit missionaries found the first permanent settlement in Indiana

1779..........George Rogers Clark captures Fort Sackville and Vincennes from the British

1787..........Indiana becomes part of the Northwest Territory

1816..........Indiana becomes the 19th state

1825..........Indianapolis becomes the state capital

1863..........General John Hunt Morgan and his Raiders invade southern Indiana

1881..........American Federation of Labor (AFL) organizes in Terre Haute

1911..........The first Indianapolis 500 race is held at the Indianapolis Motor Speedway

1937..........The Ohio River floods, causing extensive property damage

Now put yourself back in the proper year if you were the following people.

1. If you are excited because you heard that a new town had been built by missionaries, the year is _____.
2. If you are happy because the area you live in just became the 19th state, the year is _____.
3. If you are tickled to hear that a new racing event had been held, the year is _____.
4. If you are a Hoosier nervous because Confederate soldiers had raided your town, the year is _____.
5. If you are excited because American forces had captured a British fort, the year is _____.
6. If you are a French explorer fascinated by a new river you've found, the year is _____.
7. If you are a Hoosier living on the banks of the Ohio River struggling to save your home from the floodwaters, the year is _____.
8. If you are a new settler in the Indianapolis area, gratified to learn that your hometown was now the state capital, the year is _____.

ANSWER: 1.1732 2.1816 3.1911 4.1863 5.1779 6.1679 7.1937 8.1825

Indiana Investments!

Indiana banks provide essential financial services. Some of the services that banks provide include:

- They lend money to consumers to purchase goods and services such as houses, cars, and education.
- They lend money to producers who start new businesses.
- They issue credit cards.
- They provide savings accounts and pay interest to savers.
- They provide checking accounts.

Circle whether you would have more, less, or the same amount of money after each event.

1. You deposit your paycheck into your checking account.

    MORE   LESS   SAME

2. You put $1,000 in your savings account.

    MORE   LESS   SAME

3. You use your credit card to buy new school clothes.

    MORE   LESS   SAME

4. You borrow money from the bank to open a toy store.

    MORE   LESS   SAME

5. You write a check at the grocery store.

    MORE   LESS   SAME

6. You transfer money from checking to savings.

    MORE   LESS   SAME

ANSWERS: 1.more 2.more 3.less 4.more 5.less 6.same

I Am A Famous Person From Indiana—Are You?!

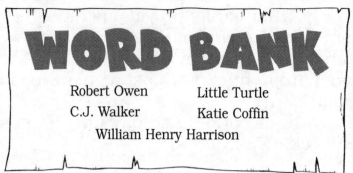

WORD BANK

Robert Owen   Little Turtle

C.J. Walker   Katie Coffin

William Henry Harrison

From the Word Bank, find my name and fill in the blank.

1. I came to Indiana as a wealthy Scottish industrialist who bought land from George Rapp in the 1800s. In 1825, I founded the New Harmony community in Indiana.
   Who am I? _____ _____

2. I was one of the nation's first female millionaires. I developed cosmetics and built my own factory in Indianapolis to produce them.
   Who am I? _____ _____ _____

3. My husband and I lived in Fountain City in the 1800s. We were members of the Underground Railroad and helped nearly 2,000 slaves escape the South
   Who are we? _____ _____ _____ _____

4. I was a Miami chief who led many raids on Indiana farms and villages. I was finally defeated at the Battle of Fallen Timbers in 1794.
   Who am I? _____ _____

5. I defeated the Shawnee Prophet at the Battle of Tippecanoe. I also ran for president in 1840 with the slogan "Tippecanoe and Tyler too."
   Who am I? _____ _____ _____

I want to be a famous Indianan for _____

_____

_____

ANSWERS: 1.Robert Owen 2.C.J. Walker 3.Katie and Levi Coffin 4.Little Turtle 5.William Henry Harrison

Indiana History Mystery Tour!

Indiana is busting at the seams with history! Try your hand at locating these historical sites, and draw the symbol for each site on the map of Indiana.

 **Lincoln Boyhood National Memorial:** near Lincoln City, where Abraham Lincoln grew up, and the burial site of his mother Nancy Hanks Lincoln

 **George Rogers Clark Memorial:** in Vincennes, site of Fort Sackville, captured by Lieutenant Colonel Clark from the British in 1779

 **Corydon Capitol:** in Corydon, preserves the first capitol building of Indiana

 **Tippecanoe Battlefield:** near Lafayette, where William Henry Harrison defeated the Indians in 1811

 **Madison:** 133 square blocks of this city are listed on the National Register of Historic Places, including the J.F.D. Lanier Mansion

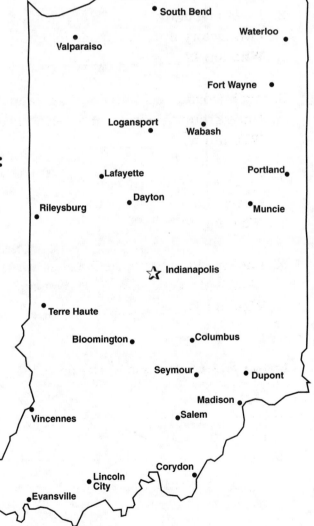

Native Hoosiers!

When the settlers arrived in Indiana, there were several Native American groups living there already. Draw a line from the group to its location on the map.

• The Miami and Kickapoo lived between the Wabash River and Lake Michigan, in the northern and northern-central parts of the state.

• The Potawatomi lived in the northernmost part of the state, just south of the St. Joseph River and east of Lake Michigan.

• The Delaware lived just north of the White River, in the eastern part of the state.

• The Shawnee lived in the southeastern part of Indiana, near the Ohio River.

It's Money in the Bank!

You spent the summer working at a concessions stand at the Indianapolis Motor Speedway, and you made a lot of money...$500 to be exact! Solve the math problems below.

TOTAL EARNED: $500.00

I will pay back my Mom this much for money I borrowed when I first started working. Thanks, Mom!

A. $20.00

    subtract A from $500

B. _____

I will give my little brother this much money for taking my phone messages while I was at work:

C. $10.00

    subtract C from B

D. _____

I will spend this much on a special treat or reward for myself:

E. $25.00

    subtract E from D

F. _____

I will save this much for college:

G. $300.00

    subtract G from F

H. _____

I will put this much in my new savings account so I can buy school clothes:

I. $100.00

    subtract I from H

J. _____

TOTAL STILL AVAILABLE
(use answer J)   _____

TOTAL SPENT
(add A, C, and E)

_____

Good Golly! Indiana Geography Word Search

Find the names of these Indiana cities in the Word Search below:

WORD BANK

BRYANT
CORYDON
EVANSVILLE
FORT WAYNE
GREENFIELD

INDIANAPOLIS
LAFAYETTE
LEAVENWORTH
MADISON

MUNCIE
NABB
NAPPANEE
SOUTH BEND
VINCENNES

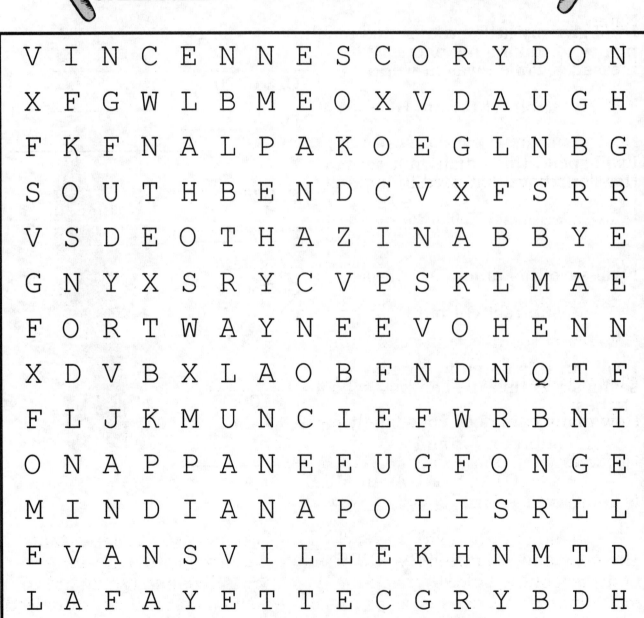

```
V I N C E N N E S C O R Y D O N
X F G W L B M E O X V D A U G H
F K F N A L P A K O E G L N B G
S O U T H B E N D C V X F S R R
V S D E O T H A Z I N A B B Y E
G N Y X S R Y C V P S K L M A E
F O R T W A Y N E E V O H E N N
X D V B X L A O B F N D N Q T F
F L J K M U N C I E F W R B N I
O N A P P A N E E U G F O N G E
M I N D I A N A P O L I S R L L
E V A N S V I L L E K H N M T D
L A F A Y E T T E C G R Y B D H
```

How Many People in Indiana?

STATE OF INDIANA

CENSUS REPORT

Every ten years, it's time for Indianans to stand up and be counted. Since 1790, the United States has conducted a census, or count, of each of its citizens. **Practice filling out a pretend census form.**

Name _____ Age ☐

Place of Birth _____

Current Address _____

Does your family own or rent where you live? _____

How long have you lived in Indiana? _____

How many people are in your family? _____

How many females? ☐   How many males? ☐

What are their ages? _____

How many rooms are in your house? ☐

How is your home heated? _____

How many cars does your family own? ☐

How many telephones are in your home? ☐

Is your home a farm? _____

Sounds pretty nosy, doesn't it? But a census is very important. The information is used for all kinds of purposes, including setting budgets, zoning land, determining how many schools to build, and much more. The census helps Indiana leaders plan for the future needs of its citizens. Hey, that's you!!

Indiana Cities!

Circle Indianapolis in red. It is our state's capital.

Circle Lafayette in blue. It's near the site of the Battle of Tippecanoe.

Circle Corydon in brown. It's where Indiana's first capital was located.

Circle Dayton in brown. The Wright brothers had a shop there.

Circle Vincennes in green. It's where the Indiana Military Museum and the George Rogers Clark National Historical Park are located.

Circle Madison in purple. More than 100 square blocks of historic homes are there.

Add your city or town to the map if it's not here. Circle it in green. Give it a 🙂 symbol to show you live there.

Oops! The compass rose is missing its cardinal directions.

Write N, S, E, W, on the compass rose.

NW   NE

SW   SE

Endangered and Threatened Indiana!

Each state has a list of the endangered species in their state. An animal is labeled endangered when it is in danger of becoming extinct. Land development, changes in climate and weather, and changes in the number of predators are all factors that can cause an animal to become extinct, or dying out completely. Today many states are passing laws to help save animals on the endangered species list.

Can you help rescue these endangered and threatened animals by filling in their names below?

1. I __ D __ __ N __   B __ __

2. G __ __ Y   B __ T

3. B __ __ __   E __ G __ __

4. C __ __ B __ __ E __ L

5. P __ __ __ G __ I __ E   F __ L __ __ N

6. P __ P __ __ G   P __ __ V __ __

Circle the animal that is extinct (not here anymore).

Hoosiers, Hum Along to ...Indiana's State Song!

"On the Banks of the Wabash, Far Away" was adopted as Indiana's state song in 1913. Both the music and the lyrics (words) were written by Paul Dresse.

"On the Banks of the Wabash, Far Away"
(first verse)

'Round my Indiana homestead wave the cornfields,
In the distance loom the woodlands clear and cool.
Oftentimes my thoughts revert to scenes of childhood,
Where I first received my lessons, nature's school.
But one thing there is missing in the picture,
Without her face it seems so incomplete,
I long to see my mother in the doorway,
As she stood there years ago, her boy to greet.

1. What wave around the Indiana homestead?

   _____

2. What do you think the word "revert" means in the third line?

   _____

3. What loom in the distance?

   _____

4. What is missing from the picture?

   _____

ANSWERS: (may vary slightly) 1. cornfields 2. to go back to, return to 3. clear and cool woodlands 4. his mother's face, his mother in the doorway

Getting Ready To Vote In Indiana!

When you turn 18, you will be eligible to vote. Your vote counts! Many elections have been won by just a few votes. The following is a form for your personal voting information. You will need to do some research to get all the answers!

I will be eligible to vote on this date _____

I live in this Congressional District _____

I live in this State Senate District _____

I live in this State Representative District _____

I live in this Voting Precinct _____

The first local election I can vote in will be _____

The first state election I can vote in will be _____

The first national election I can vote in will be _____

The governor of our state is _____

One of my state senators is _____

One of my state representatives is _____

The local public office I would like to run for is _____

The state public office I would like to run for is _____

The federal public office I would like to run for is _____

Did you know that our state government has 50 senators?

No, but I do know we have 100 representatives!

Indiana's State Seal

Indiana's state seal shows three hills in the center, with one tree on the left and two trees on the right. Fourteen rays come out of the sun that's setting behind the hills, one ray for each of the original 13 colonies, and the 14th ray for Indiana. A woodsman with an axe is on the right, and a buffalo is jumping over a log to the left. On the ground are shoots of blue grass, and above the center of the seal are the words "Seal of the State of Indiana." The year 1816 is shown on the bottom of the seal, which was the year of Indiana's statehood. Diamonds with dots and tulip tree leaves are on either side of the date.

Color the state seal.

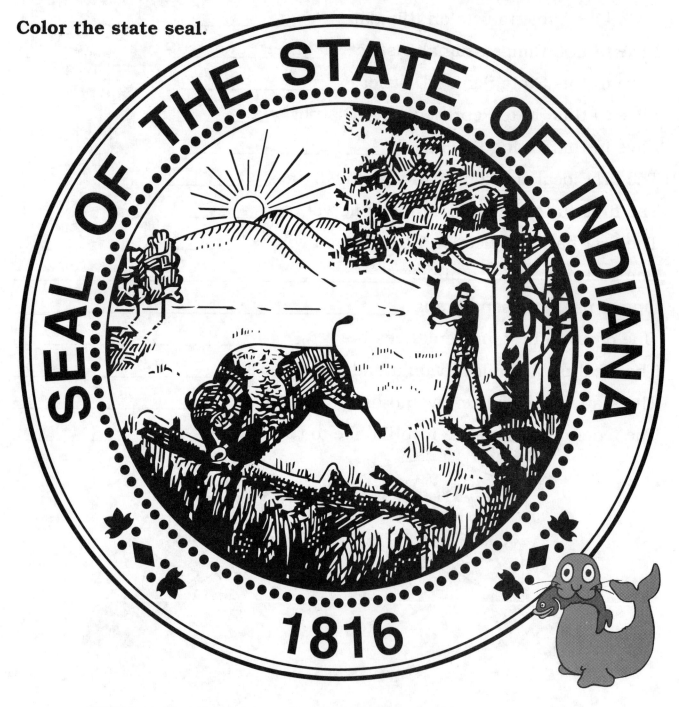

Animal Scramble!

Unscramble the names of these animals you might find in your Indiana backyard.

Write the answers in the word wheel around the picture of each animal.

1. *kipchnum* Hint: She can store more than a hundred seeds in her cheeks!

2. *ethiw dleait ered* Hint: He raises the underside of his tail to signal danger!

3. *nrocoac* Hint: He has very sensitive "fingers" and uses them to find food.

4. *ntseare ttoncoliat bitbra* Hint: She would love to eat the cabbages in your garden!

5. *yarg lquiersr* Hint: He scurries around all day, burying and digging up acorns!

A Quilt Of Many Counties!

Indiana has 92 counties.
Every city or town in
Indiana belongs to a
county.

- **Label your county.
  Color it red.**
- **Label the counties that
  touch your county.
  Color them blue.**
- **Now color the rest of
  the counties.**

Hoosier Halfsies!

How many of these two-name Indiana places can you match? You might need a map or an atlas to help you figure them out. Draw a line from each town's first half to its second half.

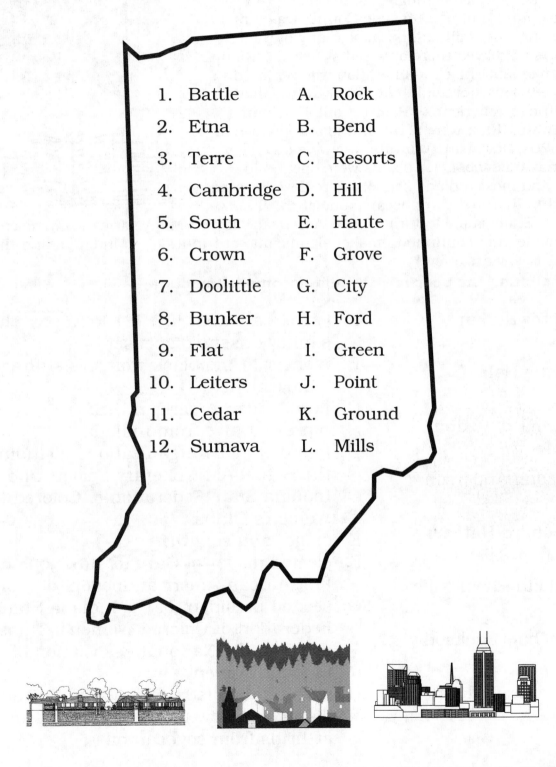

1. Battle   A. Rock
2. Etna   B. Bend
3. Terre   C. Resorts
4. Cambridge   D. Hill
5. South   E. Haute
6. Crown   F. Grove
7. Doolittle   G. City
8. Bunker   H. Ford
9. Flat   I. Green
10. Leiters   J. Point
11. Cedar   K. Ground
12. Sumava   L. Mills

ANSWERS: 1.K 2.I 3.E 4.G 5.B 6.J 7.L 8.D 9.A 10.H 11.F 12.C

Contributions by Indiana's African-Americans

The 1851 Indiana constitution forbade blacks from entering the state, but thousands of escaping slaves still traveled through Indiana using the Underground Railroad. Wayne County was a main stop along this Railroad, because many of the Quakers who lived there opposed slavery. Although the ban against black immigration was removed in 1881, tensions were still high between Indianans and African-Americans. Racist groups including the Ku Klux Klan were active in Indiana politics in the 1920s, but lost power after a few years. The first Indiana schools for blacks were opened in 1869, and most Indiana schools were desegregated by 1949. In 1967, Gary became one of the first major U.S. cities to elect an African-American mayor. Many African-Americans have made, and continue to make, significant contributions to Indiana, and the world. Below are a few.

Try matching the people with their accomplishments.

1. Percy Julian

2. Katie Hall

3. Richard Saxton

4. Naomi Anderson

5. Richard Hatcher

6. Lillian Thomas Fox

7. Michael Jackson

8. Minnie Taylor Scott

A. earned a patent in 1981 for a pay phone sanitary tissue dispenser

B. pioneer in the black women's suffrage movement

C. first African-American U.S. representative from Indiana

D. founded many organizations including the Bethel AME Literary Society and Indiana State Federation of Colored Women's Clubs

E. singer and songwriter

F. elected mayor of Gary in 1967; one of the first African-American mayors of a big city

G. second president of the Indiana State Federation of Colored Women's Clubs; active in the National Association of Colored Women

H. studied chemistry at DePauw University; discovered how to make a treatment for arthritis from soybean oil

ANSWERS: 1.H 2.C 3.A 4.B 5.F 6.D 7.E 8.G

Indiana'll Give You a Sporting Chance!

The Hoosier State is well-known for its high-quality high school and college basketball, football, and wrestling teams. Famous Hoosier hoopsters include the Indiana Pacers, the Indiana Hoosiers, and the "Milan Miracle" of 1954 that was the basis for the 1987 movie "Hoosiers." The University of Notre Dame's Fighting Irish are a respected college football team, and the Indianapolis Colts flourish on the field every football season.

Use the clues you've been given to figure out who these Hoosier sports greats are!

1. He was Indiana University's controversial and fiery basketball coach from 1971-2000, during which time IU won 11 Big 10 Conference titles. He also coached gold-medal teams in the 1979 Pan American Games and the 1984 Olympic Games.

   $+ \text{ t } - \text{ b }$ $=$ _____

2. They were Notre Dame's all-American backfield, and given this nickname by sportswriter Grantland Rice in 1924.

   4 $+$ $+$ **men** $=$ _____

3. He was a University of Notre Dame football player, and later the head coach who led the Fighting Irish in an amazing number of victories between 1918 and 1930. He was considered a football innovator in every way.

   K $+$ $+$ **E** $+$ $+$ **NE** $=$ _____

4. He was a French Lick basketball superstar who then played for 13 years for the Boston Celtics. He then returned to Indiana to coach the Indiana Pacers in 1997 and was inducted into the Naismith Memorial Basketball Hall of Fame in 1998.

   Larry $+$ $=$ _____

"Dune" Fine in Indiana!

Believe it or not, Indiana is the home of the largest sand dunes this side of the Sahara Desert! Thousands of years ago, Lake Michigan deposited sand on the beach as the water level slowly sank. Winds that blew in from the lake built up the enormous sand dunes. The Indiana Dunes National Lakeshore is situated on Lake Michigan, between Michigan City and Gary. It is a 13,000-acre (5,261-hectare) natural wonder in the middle of one of the most heavily industrialized regions in the country. It boasts lovely beaches, hiking, biking, and horseback-riding trails. However, the incredible sand dunes are what draw many visitors. Mount Baldy is a 135-foot (41-meter) tall sand dune.

Completely surrounded by the national lakeshore is the Indiana Dunes State Park. It covers 2,182 acres (883 hectares) and boasts the highest sand dune along the lakeshore—192-foot (58-meter) tall Mount Tom. If you listen carefully, sometimes you can hear a low, humming sound made by the drifting sands. These unique and soothing sounds are known locally as the music of the "singing sands."

Read each statement and use the information above to help you decide if it's FACT or FICTION. Write your answer on the line.

1. Indiana Dunes State Park is surrounded by the Indiana Dunes National Lakeshore.

_____

2. Thousands of years ago, aliens came and piled up the sand along Lake Michigan.

_____

3. The "singing sands" are actually the voices of the spirits of the first Hoosier settlers.

_____

4. Mount Baldy is more than 100 feet (30 meters) high.

_____

5. Thousands of years ago, Lake Michigan's water level sank.

_____

6. The Indiana Dunes National Lakeshore is bigger than the Sahara Desert.

_____

ANSWERS: 1.FACT 2.FICTION 3.FICTION 4.FACT 5.FACT 6.FICTION

Which Founding Person Am I?

From the Word Bank, find my name and fill in the blank.

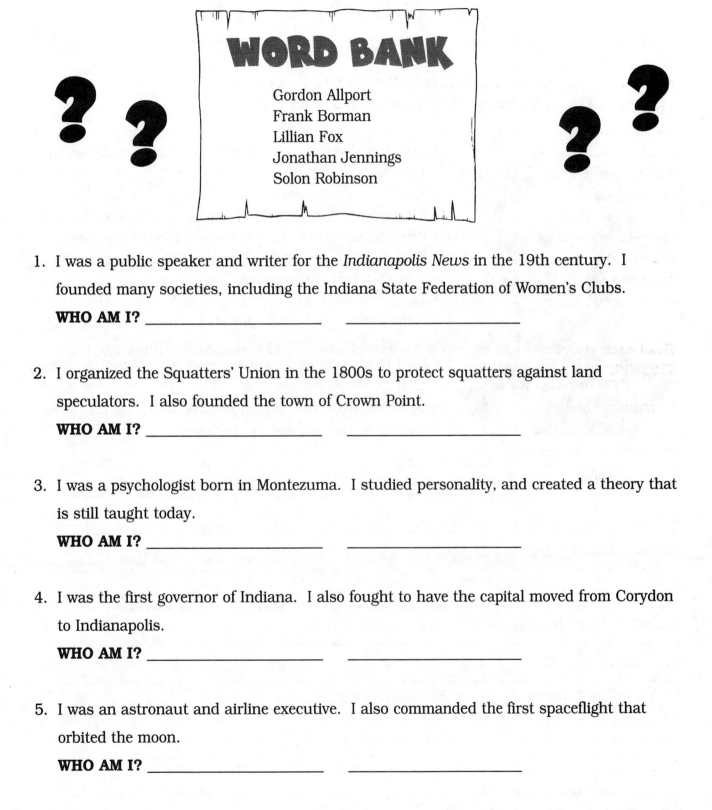

WORD BANK

Gordon Allport
Frank Borman
Lillian Fox
Jonathan Jennings
Solon Robinson

1. I was a public speaker and writer for the *Indianapolis News* in the 19th century. I founded many societies, including the Indiana State Federation of Women's Clubs.
   WHO AM I? _____ _____

2. I organized the Squatters' Union in the 1800s to protect squatters against land speculators. I also founded the town of Crown Point.
   WHO AM I? _____ _____

3. I was a psychologist born in Montezuma. I studied personality, and created a theory that is still taught today.
   WHO AM I? _____ _____

4. I was the first governor of Indiana. I also fought to have the capital moved from Corydon to Indianapolis.
   WHO AM I? _____ _____

5. I was an astronaut and airline executive. I also commanded the first spaceflight that orbited the moon.
   WHO AM I? _____ _____

ANSWERS: 1. 1.Lillian Fox 2.Solon Robinson 3.Gordon Allport 4.Jonathan Jennings 5.Frank Borman

It Could Happen–
And It Did!

These historical events from Indiana's past are all out of order.

Can you put them back together in the correct order?
(There's a great big hint at the end of each sentence.)

- Abraham Lincoln becomes the 16th president of the United States (1861)
- The Northern Indiana Toll Road opens (1956)
- Vincennes is founded (1732)
- Indiana becomes the 19th state (1816)
- Frank Borman becomes one of the first human beings to orbit the moon (1968)
- The University of Notre Dame is founded (1842)
- Indianapolis becomes the state capital (1825)
- The Shakers move to Vincennes (1805)
- Dan Quayle becomes vice-president under President George Bush (1989)
- General Anthony Wayne defeats Little Turtle at the Battle of Fallen Timbers (1794)

1. _____

2. _____

3. _____

4. _____

5. _____

6. _____

7. _____

8. _____

9. _____

10. _____

Make a Deer Skin Vest!

Native Americans wore clothing that was made from the skins of buffalo or deer. To make your deer skin vest, you will need a brown paper bag. Lay the bag flat, as shown in the picture. Cut out holes for your arms and neck. Make a long slit in one side of the bag.

Ideas for decorating your vest:

- glue buttons, glitter, and feathers on the vest

- use markers or crayons to draw Native American symbols on the vest

- make fringe at the bottom of the bag by snipping along the edges of the bag

- decorate your vest with beads, shells, etc.

Get together with your friends and have a great "pow-wow"!

Indiana People!

A state is not just towns and mountains and rivers. A state is its people! But the really important people in a state are not always famous. You may know them—they may be your mom, your dad, or your teacher. The average, everyday person is the one who helps to make the state a good state. How? By working hard, by paying taxes, by voting, and by helping Indiana children grow up to be good state citizens!

Match each Indiana person with his or her accomplishment.

1. Arthur Banta

2. Charles Austin Beard

3. Ambrose Burnside

4. Eugene Debs

5. Katie Coffin

6. Jane Pauley

7. Clement Studebaker

8. Harold Urey

A. began making wagons, then built automobiles and trucks

B. television journalist, former host of the "Today Show," now hosts "Dateline NBC"

C. considered the leading American historian of his era

D. helped thousands of slaves escape via the Underground Railroad

E. chemist who won the 1934 Nobel Prize for discovering deuterium

F. labor leader who formed the American Railway Union

G. zoologist who studied environmental effects on cave animals

H. Army officer and inventor; commanded Army of the Potomac during the Civil War

ANSWERS: 1.G 2.C 3.H 4.F 5.D 6.B 7.A 8.E

Similar Hoosier State Symbols

Indiana has many symbols including a state bird, tree, flower, flag, and seal. **Circle the item in each row that is a symbol of Indiana.**

Hoosier Roadsters!

Indiana has a long history in automobiles. Around 500 different motor vehicles have either been assembled or manufactured in more than 80 towns and cities across Indiana! On July 4, 1894, Elwood Haynes of Kokomo drove the first gas-powered clutch-driven automobile. Around the same time, several other new automobiles were developed, including the Munsen, Albanus, and DeFreet models.

The Studebaker brothers (Clement, John, Peter, and Jacob) of South Bend began experimenting with electric-powered carriages in 1897, and drove their first successful automobile in 1902. Auburn was the home of the 1920s and 1930s luxury Duesenberg cars. There were many more early Indiana automobile manufacturers, and central Indiana is still a major center for the manufacture of automobiles and automobile accessories today.

Label the parts of this automobile. Use the Word Bank to help you.

WORD BANK

steering wheel	windshield
fender	headlight
bumper	hubcap
rear view mirror	

Influential Indianans Word Wheel!

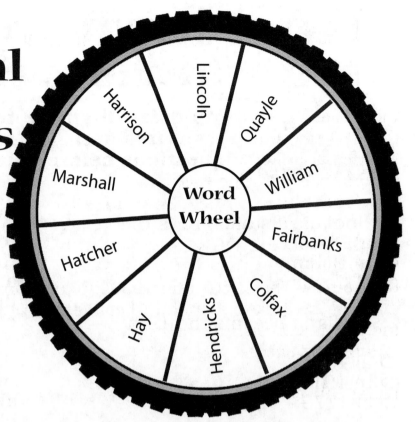

Using the Word Wheel of Indiana political figures, complete the sentences below.

1. _____ Henry Harrison became famous for winning the Battle of Tippecanoe, and also was the 9th president of the United States.
2. Benjamin _____ was a U.S. senator from 1881 to 1887, and the 23rd president of the United States.
3. Abraham _____, the 16th president, grew up in Indiana.
4. Schuyler _____ was a U.S. representative, and vice-president of the United States from 1869 to 1873.
5. Richard _____, mayor of Gary from 1968 to 1987, was one of the first African-American mayors of a large U.S. city.
6. Thomas Andrews _____ was a U.S. senator and representative, and U.S. vice-president in 1885.
7. Thomas Riley _____ was governor of Indiana from 1909 to 1913, and U.S. vice-president from 1913 to 1921.
8. James Danforth _____ was a U.S. representative and senator, and U.S. vice-president from 1989 to 1993.
9. Charles _____ was a U.S. senator from 1897 to 1905, and U.S. vice-president from 1905 to 1909.
10. John Milton _____ was the U.S. secretary of state from 1898 to 1905, and established the Open Door Policy for trade with China.

ANSWERS: 1.William 2.Harrison 3.Lincoln 4.Colfax 5.Hatcher 6.Hendricks 7.Marshall 8.Quayle 9.Fairbanks 10.Hay

Know your Indiana Facts!

Pop quiz! It's time to test your knowledge of Indiana! Try to answer all of the questions before you look at the answers.

1. Indiana's state bird is the
   - ○ a) Pigeon
   - ○ b) Robin
   - ○ c) Cardinal

2. Indiana became the 19th state in
   - ○ a) 1816
   - ○ b) 1916
   - ○ c) 1776

3. The Battle of Tippecanoe was between General Harrison and the
   - ○ a) French
   - ○ b) English
   - ○ c) Indians

4. The first permanent settlement in Indiana was at
   - ○ a) Vincennes
   - ○ b) Corydon
   - ○ c) Indianapolis

5. The capital city of Indiana is
   - ○ a) Madison
   - ○ b) Indianapolis
   - ○ c) South Bend

6. George Rogers Clark captured Fort _____ from the British.
   - ○ a) Ouiatenon
   - ○ b) Tippecanoe
   - ○ c) Sackville

7. Levi Coffin's house was a major stop on the
   - ○ a) Indiana-Ohio Railroad
   - ○ b) Indiana National Road
   - ○ c) Underground Railroad

8. Indiana's state tree is the
   - ○ a) Sugar Maple
   - ○ b) Tulip Tree
   - ○ c) Laurel

9. The Studebakers manufactured
   - ○ a) automobiles
   - ○ b) ball bearings
   - ○ c) furniture

10. The body of water northwest of Indiana is
    - ○ a) Lake Michigan
    - ○ b) Lake Erie
    - ○ c) the Atlantic Ocean

ANSWERS: 1.c 2.a 3.c 4.a 5.b 6.c 7.c 8.b 9.a 10.a

Scavenger Hunt, Indiana Style!

This is a fun hunt that includes your friends or classmates. Read the list below, find someone who has "been there and done that," get their signature and move on to the next item on your list. See how fast you can complete the scavenger hunt. Write down your answers to Part 2 and have your teacher or parent check them.

Part 1
Find someone who has:

- been to the state capitol building _____
- seen a Indiana Pacers game _____
- met a Mennonite _____
- visited the Indianapolis Motor Speedway _____
- attended the Marion Easter Pageant _____
- been to Tulipfest _____
- seen a twister _____

Part 2
Find someone who can:

- tell you Indiana's statehood date _____
- say the state motto _____
- name the state capital _____
- tell who William Henry Harrison was _____
- name a major Indiana river _____
- name the governor of Indiana _____
- name the state tree _____

Ladies and Gentlemen, Start Your Engines!

Every Memorial Day weekend, Indianapolis is filled with the mighty roar of engines. Hundreds of thousands of people crowd in to the Indianapolis Motor Speedway to watch the Indianapolis 500, the biggest and most popular race of the year. The Indy 500 not only attracts an incredible number of people to the city, but top auto racers from around the world come to compete. The prize purse for winning is $8 million! In 1994, the National Association for Stock Car Auto Racing (NASCAR) began holding its Brickyard 400 race in Indianapolis.

The Speedway itself has also been called "the Brickyard," and for good reason. It was built in 1909 from 3,200,000 paving bricks! Founders Carl Fisher, James A. Allison, Frank H. Wheeler, and Arthur C. Newby combined their money to build the 2.5-mile (4-kilometer) oval. The first Indianapolis 500 race was run in 1911.

Answer the following questions:

1. When was the Indianapolis Motor Speedway built?

_____

2. Why is it sometimes called "the Brickyard?"

_____

3. What other auto race is held at the Speedway?

_____

4. How much is the prize for winning the Indy 500?

_____

5. Who founded the Indianapolis Motor Speedway?

_____

ANSWERS: 1. 1909 **2.** it was built from 3,200,000 paving bricks **3.** the Brickyard 400 **4.** $8 million **5.** Carl Fisher, James A. Allison, Frank H. Wheeler, and Arthur C. Newby

Bio Bottles

Biography bottles are 2 or 3 liter bottles, emptied and cleaned. They are then decorated like your favorite Indiana character. They can represent someone from the past or the present like Katie Coffin, Tecumseh, or Larry Bird. Use your imagination!

Here are some items you may want to help you:

☞ 2 or 3 liter bottles

☞ scissors

☞ glue

☞ felt

☞ balloon or styrofoam ball for head

☞ paint

☞ yarn for hair

Corn on the Cob!

Corn is an important crop in Indiana. Hoosier farmers grow corn for animal feed, sweet corn for people to eat, and even popcorn! People all over the Midwest (and the rest of the country) enjoy eating grilled corn on the cob at barbecues, or just about any time! Here is a simple recipe to make your own corn on the cob, with an adult's help and a little planning ahead!

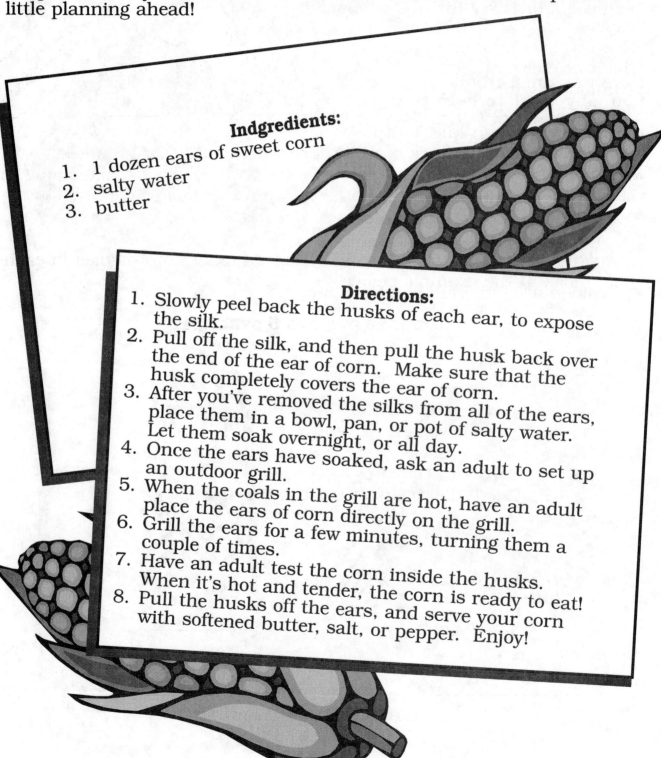

Indgredients:

1. 1 dozen ears of sweet corn
2. salty water
3. butter

Directions:

1. Slowly peel back the husks of each ear, to expose the silk.
2. Pull off the silk, and then pull the husk back over the end of the ear of corn. Make sure that the husk completely covers the ear of corn.
3. After you've removed the silks from all of the ears, place them in a bowl, pan, or pot of salty water. Let them soak overnight, or all day.
4. Once the ears have soaked, ask an adult to set up an outdoor grill.
5. When the coals in the grill are hot, have an adult place the ears of corn directly on the grill.
6. Grill the ears for a few minutes, turning them a couple of times.
7. Have an adult test the corn inside the husks. When it's hot and tender, the corn is ready to eat!
8. Pull the husks off the ears, and serve your corn with softened butter, salt, or pepper. Enjoy!

Wondrous Wyandotte Cave!

Near Leavenworth, Indiana is one of the largest caverns in the United States. Wyandotte Cave has more than 35 miles (56 kilometers) of underground passageways and chambers. One of the biggest chambers is the Rothrock Cathedral, where a 135-foot (41-meter) tall limestone "mountain" can be found! People can take tours through the vast network of natural corridors, and these tours last anywhere from 30 minutes to a whole day! Some visitors hike along the steep underground trails, and others squeeze through tight and low passages. It's truly a spelunker's paradise!

A *haiku* is a three line poem with a certain number of syllables in each line. Look at the example below:

The first line has 5 syllables
Oh, Wy/an/dotte Cave,
1   2   3   4   5

The second line has 7 syllables
Vast, dark, and mys/te/ri/ous,
1   2   3   4   5 6 7

The third line has 5 syllables
In/cred/i/ble cave!
1   2   3   4   5

Now, write your own *haiku* about the wondrous Wyandotte Cave!

_____

_____

_____

The Painted Turtle

Painted turtles live in waterways all across North America. They can grow 10 inches (25.4 centimeters) long.

"Paint" this turtle using the color key.

COLOR KEY

R = red　B = blue
Y = yellow　G = green

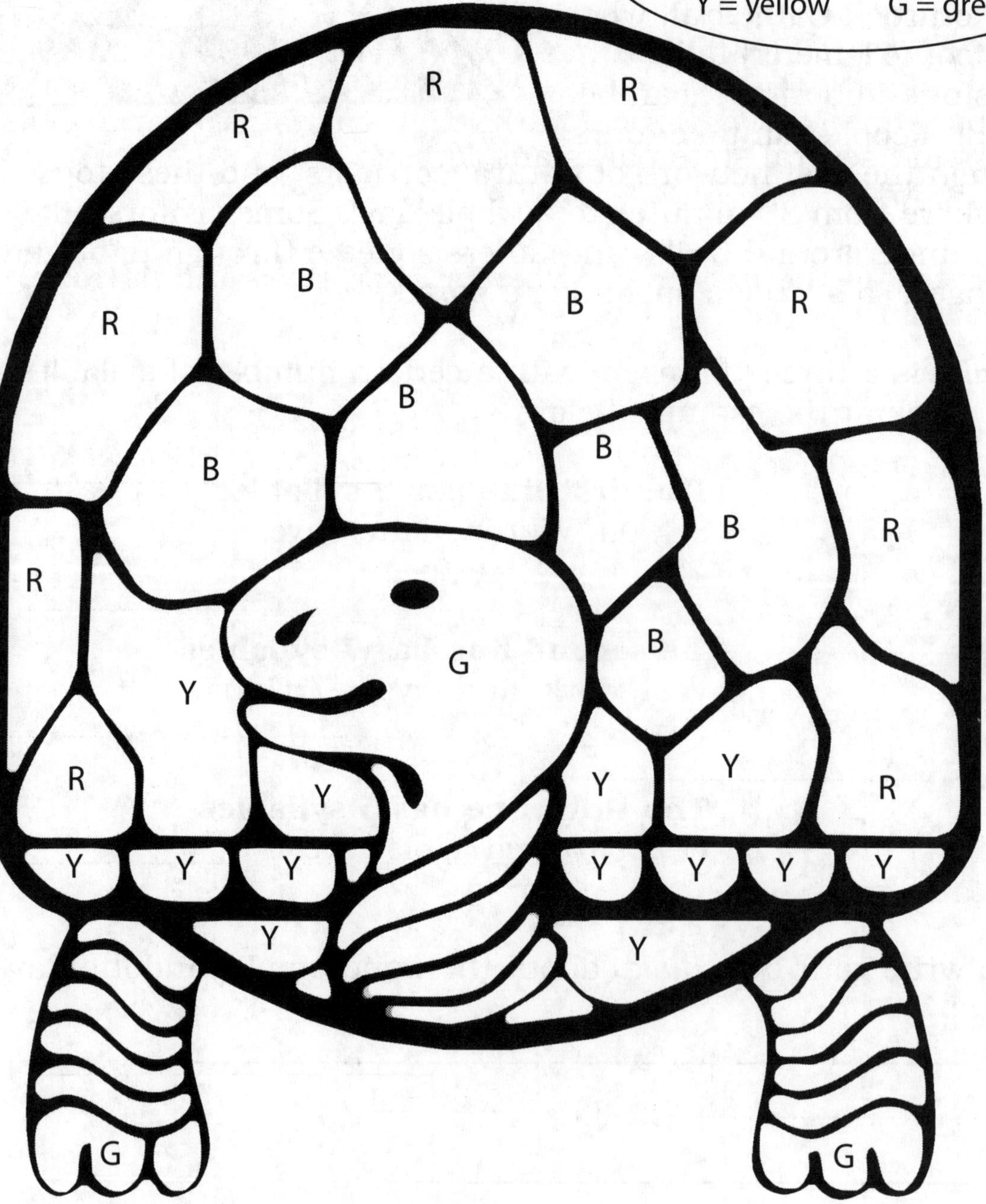

How many spots are on this turtle? ____________

ANSWER: 29

©2001 Carole Marsh/Gallopade International/800-536-2GET/www.indianaexperience.com/Page 124

Park It, Hoosier!

Indiana has made a real effort to preserve many of the natural habitats and history around the state. The Hoosier National Forest covers 193,000 acres (78,107 hectares) of land in the south-central part of the state, and the Indiana Dunes National Lakeshore has 15,010 acres (6,074 hectares) of beaches and dunes along Lake Michigan. There are also several national and state historical parks that maintain important historical sites, and several state parks and forests.

Unscramble the names of these Indiana state and national forests and parks.

1. W W E L O L O O D Y _____
   State Forest

2. N E G L A   M N O D U S _____
   _____ State Historic Site

3. N O W R B   N Y T U C O _____
   _____ State Park

4. N S G I R P   L I M L _____ _____
   State Park

5. L K R A C _____ State Forest

6. N I L O N C L   Y O B O H O D _____
   _____ National Memorial

Immense Indiana!

Indiana is the 38th largest state in the U.S. It has an area of 36,185 square miles (93,712 square kilometers).

Can you answer the following questions?

1. How many states are there in the United States?

   _____

2. This many states are smaller than our state:

   _____

3. This many states are larger than our state:

   _____

4. One mile = 5,280 ____ ____ ____ ____

   HINT:

5. Draw a "square foot" here:

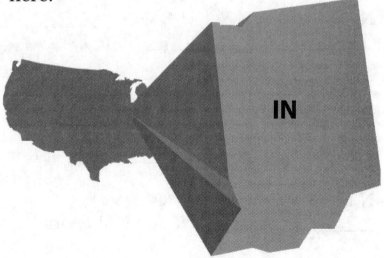

IN

Industrial Indiana Powerhouse!

During the late 19th century and early 20th century, Indiana grew very quickly. A strip of Lake Michigan shoreline called the Calumet region, where Hammond, Whiting, East Chicago, and Gary are today, was the fastest-growing area. Many large companies realized that the Calumet region was a perfect place to ship products out via Lake Michigan and built factories there. The Standard Oil Company built one of the largest oil refineries in the world in Whiting in 1889. Inland Steel opened a plant in East Chicago in 1893. In 1906, the United States Steel Corporation began building enormous steel mills along Lake Michigan, near where Gary is today.

Thousands of workers, many of them European immigrants, flooded the area looking for new jobs. By 1920, the Calumet region was one of the biggest industrial areas in North America. The region is still an industrial powerhouse and specializes in oil refining and the manufacture of steel, plastic, chemicals, and other industrial products.

Steel produced in the Calumet Region is used to make many different things. For each of these steel products, circle whether it was probably first made in the **1800s** or in the **1900s**.

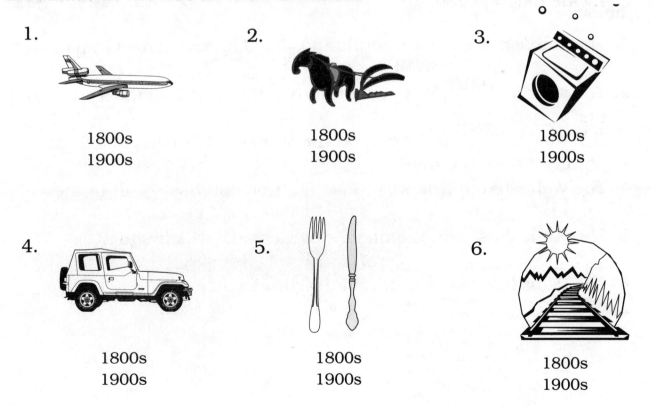

1.
1800s
1900s

2.
1800s
1900s

3.
1800s
1900s

4.
1800s
1900s

5.
1800s
1900s

6.
1800s
1900s

ANSWERS: 1.1900s 2.1800s 3.1900s 4.1900s 5.1800s 6.1800s

The Mighty Wabash!

The Wabash River rises in Ohio and flows **west** and south across the entire state of Indiana. It's part of the Indiana-**Illinois** border, where it flows into the Ohio River. The Wabash River is 512 miles (824 kilometers) in length, and with its tributaries, the river drains more than two-thirds of Indiana's **rain** and snow. Paralleling the river, the Wabash and Erie **Canal** opened in 1837 and was the longest canal ever built in the country. The popular term "Wabash Cannon **Ball**" came from a 1940s song about a train on the Wabash Railroad, which was situated alongside the river. The Wabash River is near and dear to Hoosiers' **hearts** not only because of the important role it played in Indiana's settlement, but because its beauty is memorialized in the state song. It's even Indiana's official state river!

Use the words in bold from the passage above to fill in the blanks below.

1. The Wabash River flows south and *this direction* across Indiana.
   W __ __ __

2. The river and its tributaries drain two thirds of Indiana's snow and *this*. __A __ __

3. A 1940s song about a train on the Wabash Railroad coined the phrase "Wabash Cannon B __ __ __."

4. The Wabash and Erie was the longest one of *these* built in the country. __ A __ __ __

5. The Wabash is part of Indiana's border with which state?
   __ __ __ __ __ __ __ S

6. The Wabash River is near and dear to Hoosiers' H __ __ __ __ __.

The word "wabash" is a Native American word for limestone.

ANSWERS: 1.west 2.rain 3.ball 4.canal 5.Illinois 6.hearts